W0016938

HOW NOT TO RUN A
FOOTBALL CLUB

HOW NOT TO RUN A
FOOTBALL
CLUB

**Protests, Boycotts, Court Cases –
The Inside Story of Blackpool FC**

Nathan Fogg

First published by Pitch Publishing, 2022

Pitch Publishing
9 Donnington Park,
85 Birdham Road,
Chichester,
West Sussex,
PO20 7AJ
www.pitchpublishing.co.uk
info@pitchpublishing.co.uk

© 2022, Nathan Fogg

Every effort has been made to trace the copyright.
Any oversight will be rectified in future editions at the
earliest opportunity by the publisher.

All rights reserved. No part of this book may be reproduced,
sold or utilised in any form or transmitted in any form or by
any means, electronic or mechanical, including photocopying,
recording or by any information storage and retrieval system,
without prior permission in writing from the Publisher.

A CIP catalogue record is available for this book
from the British Library.

ISBN 978 1 80150 003 6

Typesetting and origination by Pitch Publishing
Printed and bound in Great Britain by TJ Books, Padstow

Contents

For Hannah

Acknowledgements

I WOULD like to thank my girlfriend Hannah for supporting me throughout this whole process, and always being there despite being busy enough with your own work. I couldn't ask for a better partner to spend a lockdown during a global pandemic with. Next, I would like to thank my parents, Kathryn and Michael. Especially my dad for raising me as a Blackpool fan, forcing me to stick with them even when I wanted to support Burnley because all my friends did. Also, for reminding me every time we met up for a beer and would talk about the crazy twists and turns at Blackpool, 'You should have written that book you talked about Nath.' I'm glad I finally decided to. I'd like to thank my brothers, Matthew and Niall, for their support. I'd also like to thank Rachael Kay for providing some research, and Kevin Clarke for helping read through early drafts. I would also like to thank Rebeka Kay, who did nothing, but wouldn't let me get away with thanking the others but not her. I interviewed a lot of people for this book. I would like to thank anyone who took time to speak to me. There's too many to get through and some I can't mention by name due to anonymity. I need to especially thank Tim Fielding however, for providing an endless amount of help and spending many hours over several different interview sessions talking with me, and for reading through a draft version. Thank you to Jane at Pitch Publishing for believing in me and this story, and giving it a platform. Thank you to Alex Wade who provided the invaluable legal edit. Thank you to all my friends. Thanks to Adam France. Thanks to all the staff at the Fox pub in York, especially Mandy, Mica and Anna. Thank you to Brett Ormerod for being my first hero in football. Thank you to Charlie Adam for scoring that goal at Wembley. And thank you to every single Blackpool fan who sacrificed in the fight to get the club back. Everyone who boycotted and put aside the joy that watching football on a Saturday afternoon gave them, for a greater cause. Everyone who donated to the fans wrongfully sued. Everyone who turned up to protests and made their voices heard. You won.

Introduction

BLACKPOOL WERE in crisis. It was 1986. The club had long since slipped from the top of the English football pyramid and had been mired in the lower leagues ever since. The town was undergoing social and economic change. The prestige and shine of one of the UK's most booming holiday destinations was wearing away, year by year. The club followed the fortunes of its community. Fans were bitter. Some were angry. Others had grown apathetic. Their home, Bloomfield Road, was quite literally falling apart. Capacity had been slashed in half and then slashed some more due to safety concerns. It came close to being condemned several times.

The club had no money to renovate the ground. Instead, short-term fixes created a Frankenstein's monster of a stadium, with its rusty, corrugated steel exterior an eyesore on the town. The roof of the iconic Spion Kop needed urgent repairs. To save money, they had it removed and fans were left exposed to the harsh seaside elements. They chopped down the floodlights which careened in the high winds coming off the Irish Sea.

Blackpool had to take a loan from the council just to stay afloat. They had already gone cap in hand to the supporters several times over the last decade, selling shares at inflated prices to bring money in. The generosity of those loyal patrons kept the club alive, but the vultures were circling, ready to pick it apart. It was reported a retailer was interested in buying the Bloomfield Road land in order to demolish the stadium and build a supermarket. Rumours swirled over where Blackpool would find their new home, ranging from a new development down the road to a ground-share with fierce rivals Preston. The future was uncertain. The Premier League and all its glitz and glamour, which would breathe new life into English football, was still being planned in secret meetings behind closed doors. Football was in a bad place, and Blackpool came close to not seeing its bright future.

Then came an investor. A local businessman who wanted to save his childhood team from bankruptcy. Yet when Owen Oyston bought the club in 1988, relief and excitement were tempered by a great deal of suspicion. By now, Oyston was one of the most famous businessmen in Lancashire. He had the money needed to save the club from extinction, that much was clear. He told an inspirational story of growing up as the son of a miner and turning himself into a multi-millionaire. The finer points of his history are spotty. At one point it is reported he left for London to find work as an actor, living on a pint of milk every two days. He gave up and returned to Blackpool with just '£7 pounds in cash and four gallons of petrol'. The fact that the petrol was in the Jaguar he was driving is a detail left standing jarringly on its own. He went into business with his father, running an estate agency out of their home, eventually taking over ownership himself and developing it into the huge network it had become by the late 80s. Despite his success, there were some doubts about his credentials. Many of those new minor shareholders voted against his takeover.

Oyston was known as an eccentric character, parading himself in outlandish white suits on TV adverts for his estate agency. He professed his lifelong love for the club and described himself as a superfan, but few could recall ever seeing him at the ground – until he bought it. Then you couldn't miss him, when he arrived at games five minutes before kick-off in his flash sports car. His money was good, he just didn't need to use any of it to purchase the club. The price was £1.

Oyston took on the liabilities, which included the loan of nearly £200,000 from the council, but fans and local businesses had put more money in themselves, and they didn't boast to everyone in earshot that they saved the club. There were times when Owen portrayed it almost like charity, something he'd done purely out of the goodness of his own heart. This downplayed the status and power the purchase gave him. Now, he could wine and dine people and give them free tickets for a day out at the game. He could cosy up to local council members and get them on his side for the endless projects he was always trying to get off the ground. His arrival sparked a tension between owner and fans that never went away. Owen probably had saved Blackpool FC, but in doing so he had gotten his hands on an asset of great community value. Even the liabilities he'd taken on were more than offset by the value of the land he'd acquired. The sale brought with it not just the stadium and team, but the training ground, a nightclub neighbouring the stadium, and some other land that could all easily be sold – and later was – for profits in redevelopment schemes. Still, nobody could deny Owen went on to put his money where his mouth was to try to turn around the club's fortunes.

In 1971 Blackpool were playing in the old First Division, where they had competed for most of the last half-century. Ten years later, after a stunning decline on the pitch, they suffered their third relegation in a decade to fall all the way down to the Fourth Division, the basement of the Football League. It had been a spectacular crash, culminating in the embarrassment of having to apply for re-election in 1983. They survived the process and were even able to climb the table and win promotion two years later, but these were still well and truly the dark days of Blackpool Football Club. This was the scene when Owen Oyston took over. After 17 years away from the top division, any idea that Blackpool were 'too big' to stay down had surely dissipated long ago. Now their noses were just being rubbed in it. Many fans had given up hope almost altogether. So, when Oyston came in with bombastic rhetoric and grand schemes for change, some were simply too jaded to believe him.

It didn't help that his biggest plan was a super stadium that could house 50,000 fans, with a retractable pitch and roof, a built-in 'coliseum' of shops, along with a bowling alley and a concert venue. It was announced with great bluster to a bemused audience. Blackpool fans didn't need a high-tech coliseum, only 3–4,000 were even attending games by 1990. In a football world shaken to its core by the recent tragedies of the Bradford City fire and Hillsborough, they just wanted a stadium that was safe for them. As the years went by, nothing ever came, and Bloomfield Road fell into more and more neglect. It became clear that the new stadium was just a pipe dream. Oyston lost whatever credibility he had. The money he was spending on the pitch wasn't getting results either. Throughout the 90s Blackpool splashed some cash, but none of it ever really got them anywhere. Record transfer Chris Malkin, bought for £275,000, flopped. Andy Preece and Gary Brabin arrived for £200,000 each and had a greater impact on the pitch, but were still unable to help the team climb the leagues. It would be wrong not to point out that the club did manage to generate plenty of money from selling players, and in fact, by the time the decade was over, they had made a healthy £600k profit on all their dealings in the transfer market. But most of the investment was going into the ballooning wage bill.

The fans were not satisfied. They were left devastated when Oyston sacked beloved manager Billy Ayre, who they had developed an especially close relationship with. His successors, Sam Allardyce and Gary Megson, may have boasted better win percentages, but ultimately fell short of their end goal of promotion. At times they played a turgid brand of football that only alienated supporters further. Nigel Worthington followed with an even more negative style, but this time without the results behind him to justify it.

In 1996, Oyston was sentenced to prison for raping a 16-year-old girl. Oyston was 57 at the time of the assault. The court heard about his friendship with Peter Martin, who ran a modelling agency in Manchester, and was later himself sentenced to 20 years imprisonment for raping and assaulting several teenage girls he had groomed. Martin fed his trainee models 'hypnotic pills' under the disguise of vitamin and slimming supplements and preyed on their vulnerable state of wellbeing. Sat in court to watch the day he was sentenced was the victim Owen had raped. Owen had carried on a relationship with several of the models over a number of years. The night it happened, Martin had invited Oyston to a dinner, with many models from his agency attending. They decided to move on to Owen's house at Claughton Hall afterwards, and Martin drove over with Owen and the 16-year-old girl in the back. During the journey, Owen grabbed her hand and made her masturbate him, then pushed her head down and forced her to give him oral sex. Later in the evening, he took her to his room and had sex with her while she lay still, unable to consent, terrified of what had happened and because Martin was waiting outside.

Owen used his influence as owner of the *Miss World* beauty pageant and connection to the modelling agency to lure in young women. He lavished them with gifts and money. He targeted teenage women who were trying to make it in a cut-throat industry and told them he had the keys. Most of his behaviour was not illegal. However, after hearing the events of that night, the jury found him guilty of rape. He was given a six-year sentence and was released early after just three and a half years.

Through various appeals in court and to anybody who would listen, Owen cried conspiracy. It went all the way to the top of the Conservative government, who he alleged wanted to put away a long-time Labour supporter and donor. He managed to convince a good many Blackpool fans, using his position as owner to spread his propaganda. He produced a dossier of what he called 'evidence' regarding the cover-up and had parts printed out at games and passed around. But even people close to him didn't buy it.

The Court of Appeal discussed his parole case. While noting that he steadfastly maintained his innocence and refused to accept his guilt, they wrote, 'It is common ground that the risk of offending arose substantially from the respondent's lifestyle ... If his lifestyle were to change, the risk of his offending would be greatly reduced. The Parole Board accepts that there was considerable evidence before the Board as to a possible change in lifestyle by the respondent and that the evidence was relevant to an assessment of the risk to which the members of the public were subject.'

The consensus description from all those who knew him was that upon his release, Owen's lifestyle largely stayed the same. Right the way through to his last days at the club two decades later, if you were in the sponsors' lounge for a game, you'd inevitably see Owen walk past with women surrounding him. He invited his female acquaintances to games and paraded them in front of guests. The 'strong family bonds' he had which the court took into consideration did not seem to extend much longer after his release. To many observers, he seemed to maintain a lurid fixation on being seen with attractive women, many years his junior, on his arm. Where others saw shame, he apparently saw symbols of wealth and power. There was no great change in behaviour, but even if the Court of Appeal suggested this increased the risk of offending, Oyston did not. There were no further allegations made against him, and nothing illegal about his future actions. However, it did make those close to him question, if his conviction had been the result of a conspiracy to set him up by Conservative powerbrokers, why *didn't* he change his lifestyle? Why *did* he put himself into similar positions where entrapment could follow again?

Behind his back, people sniggered at his behaviour after release. While it didn't stray against the law, it was still an embarrassment for all those associated with the club, even his own family. When arranging tickets at away games, members of staff felt a twinge of humiliation whenever asked to give names for the people they were purporting to be club officials, as they listed off names like 'Candice' and 'Kylie' – women he had met the night before. Owen bragged that he had an open tab in every bar in Lancashire and would sit in a booth and send bottles of champagne to a table of girls young enough to be his great-granddaughters. A worker at one such establishment recalled his disgust when he saw Owen, in his 70s by then, with his tongue down an 18-year-old girl's throat. A local car dealership says it became familiar with routine visits from young girls asking to buy a car, explaining, 'Mr Oyston at the football club is paying for it.'

Despite his conviction, his money and influence brought about more partnerships with fashion companies. In 2015, *The Mirror* reported that four models had locked themselves away from him after realising who he was when they were working at his house for a photo shoot. They were terrified to learn they were staying over for the night, rather than at a hotel. Owen asked to extend the shoot and for the girls to take photos while wearing his clothing; they declined as politely as they could. At dinner he made sure to seat himself next to them. He asked one for her number, but she again declined. 'We huddled together in one room and locked the door. It was the longest night of my life,' another said afterwards. While it occurred many years later, it was a story that didn't seem compatible with the lifestyle change he promised he would undertake.

His wife, Vicki Oyston, stood by her husband during the trial. She defiantly proclaimed that she believed he was innocent. She was forced to accept the string of affairs Owen had carried on for several years, which he had admitted to in court, but she stayed loyal to him. She remarked, 'Once they have made the decision to do something, they shouldn't blame someone else for it … I have been out with Owen and seen people homing in on him. When people are rich and well-known, other people want to be alongside them. It must be very difficult for a man not to take what's on offer.' While helping on his appeal, she gave an interview to *The Mirror* where she seemed to suggest that they could have done more to challenge the idea that the victim 'was dependant and vulnerable'. 'She was obviously a troubled person who had a strong impact on the court. She was shaking and rocking and breaking down intermittently. We didn't want to add to her problems. We've had a lot of regrets about that since … But this isn't about her sexual history. It's about the false picture she painted of her life by saying she wasn't allowed to contact her parents or have money to spend.' Vicki's patience did eventually wear thin, and she separated from Owen in 2004. Speaking now, while standing by her statement that many women threw themselves at her husband because he was a millionaire, she described her thoughts on the case as 'less clear'.

Vicki had previously been a director at the club, but while Owen was behind bars she was handed the keys and promoted to chairman – she didn't allow anyone to call her chairwoman. Football was not kind to Vicki, and neither were Blackpool fans. There were regular 'Oyston out' protests, not nearly as vociferous and vocal as the demonstrations and boycott that would come later, but still laced with a distrust and hatred of the family. It had become deep-rooted in sections of the fanbase. At games, Vicki would sit at the back of the stand, within touching distance of the fans. The directors' seating wasn't elevated or protected behind glass windows. This close proximity brought many nasty encounters, as supporters would inevitably turn their ire to the ownership as the team laboured on the pitch.

It was an especially ugly time for women in football. No other club in the Football League had a woman in charge, and misogyny was a daily routine. In 1988, back when she was a director, Blackpool played a game away at Tranmere. As is custom, Vicki wanted to mingle with the Tranmere directors, so she made her way to the boardroom before the game. When she arrived, the door was closed on her and she was denied entry. No women were allowed. Boardrooms were still the inner sanctum for old white men to share drinks and smoke cigars and make sexist jokes at the expense of their wives. Tranmere dropped their policy when Blackpool lodged an official complaint and the local Labour council threatened to withdraw funds they were loaning the club.

Most visits to away grounds were friendly, but the unfriendly incidents were especially so. Vicki recalled Port Vale giving Blackpool an advance warning, 'If she comes to the match she won't be allowed in the boardroom.' The message hadn't been passed to her, so she went expecting a warm welcome. As she entered, each male director turned their backs and refused to talk to her. She described another incident at Huddersfield, where a greeter was welcoming visitors. She overheard him say, 'I'm watching out here, there's one of *those* coming today. This is what I'd do to her if I saw her,' before he motioned spitting on the floor and rubbing it in with his shoe.

The sexism Vicki faced was real, and she faced a good deal of it from the Blackpool fans too. But they weren't without good reason to want her and her husband out. The team was stagnating. Owen was in prison. They had been subjected to lower-league football, in a stadium barely safe enough to stay open, for far too long. Anti-Oyston songs became more and more regular at games. Fans held a march around the Bloomfield Road stadium carrying a tangerine coffin, decrying the slow death of the club. Another march led fans all the way to Vicki's house.

In stepped a consortium led by another local millionaire, David Haythornthwaite. Haythornthwaite had spotted a way in when negotiations between Owen Oyston and McAlpine, the construction company, broke down over land to be used for the proposed new stadium. He took up new negotiations himself and publicly promised he could deliver where Owen had failed. Fans were eager to hear him out. There were real concerns that Bloomfield Road would soon fail to qualify for a safety certificate. In a game on Christmas Eve 1998, a strong gale caused damage to the now vastly reduced 1,500-capacity Spion Kop, forcing its complete closure for over a month.

The Oystons had failed, and a new investor was capturing attention. This was when Owen and Vicki's son, 30-year-old Karl Oyston, entered the scene. Vicki was planning her exit and anointed Karl as her successor. Owen didn't want Karl anywhere near the top job; the two had always had a strained relationship. Karl suspected his father would rather have given the role to almost anybody else. But his demands were ignored. Vicki made the decision and there was little he could do from his prison cell. Vicki and Karl went to meet Haythornthwaite to discuss his proposed offer to buy the club, which he'd proudly presented through the local media.

Karl bristled. He thought of Haythornthwaite as little more than a chancer, writing cheques in the press he couldn't actually cash. His opinion turned out to be wrong, as Haythornthwaite later went on to plough cash into neighbours AFC Fylde. However, Vicki was similarly unimpressed. Her view lowered throughout the meeting as she said he refused to speak to her and addressed only Karl. 'He was the most sexist man I ever met,' she recalled, an accusation which bemused Haythornthwaite. He explained he had no idea who Karl even was until he arrived at the meeting – 20 minutes after it started – and he had always intended to have dialogue with Vicki. Either way, the meeting didn't last long, as Karl stormed off. 'You're wasting your time and you're wasting my time,' he said as he left. Soon afterwards, Karl took over from Vicki on a full-time basis. He carried on in his role as chairman for 19 years. During his time in charge he went on to oversee some huge success for the club, followed by an even more spectacular fall. Along the way he became the most controversial chairman a British football club has ever had.

Karl officially took over in 1999. Any promise of a new super stadium had by now faded into history. The accounts for the Blackpool FC holding company – which owned the football team and attached properties – showed just how much money was being flushed down the drain. Over the previous five years they had lost, on average, £822,000 per year and had net liabilities of £4.3m. Blackpool fans didn't like the Oystons and Karl didn't much like the fans either. The stories of awful incidents his mother had faced were well known around the town. Of being spat at on more than one occasion, of leaving the stadium late at night and running away from a small pack of men to get to her car safely. It's easy to see why Karl – who had no interest in football and thought it was a foolish vanity project for his dad to ever own a club – came on to the scene immediately in confrontation with the fanbase.

Nobody was happy. Karl had been to five or six football games in his entire life. Where others saw 'passion' and 'loyalty', he saw an amorphous mob. He cared little for what the club meant to the thousands of people who came weekly to Bloomfield Road, who just wanted to see their team prosper, whoever was in charge. His grandparents had suggested his name after Karl Marx, but he didn't take after him. He didn't understand the role a football team could play in a downtrodden, working-class community. He saw a string of companies owned by his dad, some very successful, propping up one other business – Blackpool FC, which lost money every year. For this pleasure, his family were hated. His dad was in prison and his mum had left because she couldn't take it any more. Karl's one and only purpose, he felt, was to cut costs and get the business back on an even footing.

Karl was always an outsider coming in trying to fix a mess. As he looked around the footballing landscape, he could not understand how other chairmen were allowing their clubs to be run. He felt no pressure to fit in and had no interest in copying what everyone else was doing. Football was broken. He hadn't played when he was younger, he'd never had a job in football before, and he didn't have contacts or loyalties to anybody but himself and his family's money. He didn't seem to care for anyone else's feelings or how he might upset the natural order. When he saw his manager sub on three players in the 90th minute when leading 3-0, he realised he was only doing so because it triggered an appearance bonus for the players. This was a tradition many managers did at clubs everywhere. It was just an accepted way of doing things. Not any more. Karl changed the rules on new contracts so that a player's appearance money would be pro rata. If he had a £90 appearance fee and came on for the last minute, he got £1. The player being subbed off got £89. He moved away from win and draw bonuses to straight-up promotion bonuses. He figured the team might win more games in an otherwise stronger league season but still end up in the same position they were last year, costing him more money for nothing.

He budgeted every year for the worst-case scenario. For poor attendances, lacklustre merchandise sales, to get knocked out in the first round of every cup. He limited spending in accordance with that figure when planning for the season ahead. This immediately placed a target on his own back. Football supporters feed on a diet of optimism and hope. Karl could decry this all he wanted, but stagnation was ill reward for those customers turning up each game and putting so much money into the club's coffers year after year. Many were more financially literate than he would give them credit for, and he wrongly tried to paint all naysayers as reckless gamblers who would happily fritter away millions, when what they really wanted was to not be told over and over again that simply scraping by was the best they should hope for. His common tactic when it came to recruitment for the new season was to wait until the last few days in the transfer window in the hope of a cheaper deal, with the added benefit of saving on an extra few weeks' wages. Sometimes he would wait until after the deadline closed, hoping to pick up free agents, or what he dubbed 'the flotsam and jetsam'. It was an insult to the fans he relied on. What made it worse was that no matter how much money the club had in the bank, his strategy never changed.

Perhaps the most contentious change was dropping player salaries after the final game of the season to the national minimum wage level. They still got the same yearly salary, just more up front during the season and then as little as legally possible during the off-season. The move was motivated by a desire to force players who didn't have a future at the club to leave as soon as possible, rather than waiting until August to run down their contract. Karl *never* wanted a single penny wasted on a player who didn't deserve it. If a player was on a three-year contract and not playing a single minute, why should he get the same pay as everybody else? What if they were happy collecting their wages and didn't want to leave? What Oyston's cunning plan may not have accounted for, of course, was that the good players who had better offers elsewhere were also desperate to leave.

The changes continued. Blackpool were the only club around to make players pay their own FA registration fee. They were the first team to put options in their contracts, meaning almost every single new signing had an extra year on their deal that the club could trigger at its discretion. A three-year deal became a two-plus-one deal, and Blackpool could decide whether they stayed for that extra year or not. The move was copied, and such options are now commonplace throughout football. Wages would rise and fall drastically dependent on the division. Bloated contracts that clubs couldn't get rid of had become such a problem in football that the Premier League devised 'parachute payments' for relegated teams. Blackpool themselves had suffered greatly from this in the 1970s when they fell sharply through the divisions from the top tier, unable to get rid of high-earning players. That wasn't going to happen under Karl Oyston. He doubled wages on promotion (provided the player had played enough games) but would halve them again on relegation. Years later, when Blackpool were promoted to the Premier League and subsequently relegated, they were the beneficiaries of tens of millions in such parachute payments. Karl joked to colleagues that they didn't even need them.

Along the way he was met with fierce opposition. Gordon Taylor, the head of the Professional Footballers' Association, called his contracts 'slave labour'. Yet most football fans would consider some of the changes fairly reasonable. The £90-a-week wages during the summer was always the most controversial move, but things like team options and bonus-laden, incentive-based contracts seemed to have great benefits. It protected the club from ever being saddled with burdensome contracts. It ensured players had to earn playing time to reap the full rewards of their deals. Those who weren't in the first team wouldn't want to hang around and therefore wouldn't take up club salary costs. There were downsides, of course, and Blackpool missed out on an endless number of players due to competitors offering much better rates, even from lower divisions.

In response to Taylor's accusation in the media, Karl sent a list of bullet points to all the chairmen in English football, listing in detail all the unique quirks of his contracts. He was completely open about his approach. More and more clubs started to copy him. Later, Karl was even elected on to the Football League board by his peers. The football world only grew into a bigger and bigger financial beast, one which Karl could not understand, but privately many other chairmen were envious of the way he operated. The biggest change of all was the long-overdue redevelopment of Bloomfield Road. With money from Owen Oyston, now out of prison, along with a hefty grant from the Football League, new, modern stands were built after the turn of the century. On their opening, a large banner presented by a group of fans read 'Thank You Karl'. In typical fashion, the area where the now-demolished South Stand once lay was left empty for nearly a decade. 'We don't even fill the other stands, why should we pay to build another?' Karl argued.

Karl's stringent financial planning managed to drag Blackpool on to a more even financial keel rather quickly. In the five seasons prior to him taking over, the club had lost a total of £4,113,351. The wage bill had doubled throughout the 90s as they threw money at failed attempts at promotion. It barely inched upwards once Karl took hold of the purse strings. In the five years after he took over, losses stood at a much more manageable £174,810. And this was without any great boost in attendance, or improved league position. In 2002 the club was even able to turn a healthy profit, thanks largely to the record sale of fan-favourite Brett Ormerod to Southampton for £1.75m.

But the way he managed money only tells half the picture of Karl Oyston. The other half is how he managed people. Through testimony of several who worked with him or were close to him, he was a bully. He could start off sweet and charming, but many relationships he had ended with a falling-out due to his uncooperative and harsh manner. Staff salaries were desperately low. Whenever a person left it created a new opportunity to cut the positional pay for the next hire. He tried to run the club with absolute rule, although lower-level staff did their best to work around him and squeeze money out of the budget for small improvements where they could get them. Anyone, at any time, was at risk of facing a tirade of abuse. He was described as 'detesting' footballers, thinking they were all overpaid, overrated and greedy. These were lower-league footballers he was dealing with, two decades ago. None had as much money as his own family did, and all arguably had to work much harder to get where they were than he had, born into a rich family and given control of several multi-million-pound businesses. Shortly after he took over, he took an employee out for a spin in the Ferrari he drove. While they were out, in an off-the-cuff comment, he said 'I've no interest in football, I'd like to be a pig farmer instead.'

He had a small but close group of staff around him who stayed for years, longevity he could point to as evidence of a productive, healthy work environment. But staff who were willing to speak were unanimous in their portrayal of an almost cartoonishly cold-hearted businessman who didn't care about people. That includes Derek Spence, an ex-Pool player who had built the Community Trust, an organisation attached to the club that used football as a means of uplifting the community. They would go into schools and work on local NHS health initiatives, aiming to use the most famous business in Blackpool as a beacon. After two decades of service, he had built a charity from nothing to one that regularly pulled in hundreds of thousands of pounds in funding. He eventually left, citing a toxic atmosphere, saddened he hadn't fulfilled his dream to carry on building the legacy for even more years to come. It was only afterwards that he realised the damage working daily with Oyston had done to his mental health, and he undertook four years of counselling to help him cope with the stress and anxiety which a therapist warned him was 'through the roof'.

Despite a huge number of offices being available in the stadium, for many years the Trust were made to work out of a converted garage connected to Spence's house in Fleetwood. The phones at Bloomfield Road directed to their office, so people thought they were housed at Blackpool FC, but Karl wouldn't actually allow them to work there. Those in the Trust believed he had no interest in the work they were doing, with no regard at all for what a positive force it could be in the town. When they did have meetings at the ground, Spence alleged Karl used his position of authority to bully him, and thought being Irish made him an 'easy target'. He had a hearing aid which, as is common with daily use, would sometimes run out of batteries. According to Spence, it would occasionally run out in meetings and he would have to apologise for not being able to hear as well, and at that moment Karl would intentionally barrage him with questions left, right and centre in order to embarrass him. Karl denied this story, claiming Spence was a 'liability' with an axe to grind. Other staff members who left were reluctant to talk about him on record, describing him as vindictive and worried about what consequences they could face for speaking out. When stories of complaints were put to Karl, he continually batted them away as personal grievances, which should raise its own question as to why so many would have them.

Karl loved the daily sparring battles that came with running the club. His first managerial hire was Steve McMahon, who won them promotion from the bottom division but had probably taken them as far as he could by 2004. McMahon put in a letter of resignation, claiming he was tired of football and in need of an extended break – although Karl happened to know he was already talking with Oldham about their managerial position. Karl warned him if he did have a change of heart and signed with Oldham, he would owe Blackpool a pre-agreed figure on his contract, about £30,000. McMahon ripped up his resignation halfway through a press conference, with local and national media in attendance ready to report on his departure. He lashed out at Karl, warning him 'I'm going to make your life a fucking misery', in a tantrum. Towards the end of the season, with the club already safe from relegation, he started picking players from the youth team to play. They got turned over in games of men v boys. None were ready for that level and there was little hope any ever would be. Karl refused to budge. In return, he told McMahon he wasn't going to pick up the options of his key players and would let them leave on a free transfer in the summer. McMahon blinked, and agreed to leave. Oyston picked up the options three days later.

In 2008, Blackpool were trying to sign defender Alex Baptiste from Mansfield Town. Karl and a bunch of other chairmen were in Portugal for a summer conference, which essentially amounted to a knees-up retreat. Mansfield chairman Keith Haslam wanted £25,000, but Karl wanted to bring the price down. Haslam pointed at Cardiff chairman Peter Ridsdale, who was stood by the hotel pool in a full suit, and said, 'If you push him in, you can have him for ten.' He didn't hesitate. He ran straight over and pushed Ridsdale into the water. Haslam was good on his word and they brought the price down. It was a no-brainer if it meant saving a bit of money. When he was negotiating the deal to sell Brett Ormerod, he wanted to reduce the amount he would have to pay Ormerod's former club, Accrington Stanley, who were due a 40 per cent cut of his sell-on fee. Karl called them and demanded they lower it, or else he would refuse to sell. They either didn't have the financial means or the foresight to call his bluff and agreed. The smart gamesmanship earned Blackpool a higher profit.

He offered no such leeway when he was on the selling end. Years later, when top Premier League clubs rang with interest in Charlie Adam, Karl let them know his asking price was £6m. 'Oh we can only do £5.5m,' one would reply. 'Fuck off then, it's £6m,' was his answer. Then they would come back with a new offer, 'What about £5.75m?' His stern response never wavered. 'No, it's £6m.' Having a no-nonsense attitude and refusing to entertain anything less than the asking price are hardly criticisms, but it was in negotiations with players and their representatives where things usually got more abrasive. That's if he showed up at all, as on several occasions managers and players have claimed he had such little appetite for hearing out the other side he skipped out on meetings entirely. One agent described what Karl was like, 'He was so rude. Lots of players and their agents just thought, "I'm not dealing with him." It was almost like you're a piece of shit, you're a piece of trash. Yes, I'll have you here, this is what you get. Take it or leave it. It was that kind of behaviour. You can't deal with people like that.'

From his point of view, he described agents as 'bloody useless' and professed his refusal to pay them, although he often did, just in disguised ways – with scouting or consultant fees. One source described the scene one day when he was visiting Karl at the stadium. He noticed a player in reception, waiting with his agent. 'Are you going to sign this guy then?' he asked, to which he claims Karl replied, 'No, I'm not, he wants £15,000 a week. I'm just gonna make them sit out there, the robbing bastards.' He left them waiting six hours. Karl had a back door in his office, a fire escape that led out on to the concourse, and he could walk right past waiting visitors, then go into his office and walk back out the other side. Another person inside the club corroborated a similar story, although Karl denied he would purposefully leave agents waiting, but only because 'one of the few good bits of the job was telling them to get lost'. Karl's war on agents was a mostly one-man crusade. It's a common refrain from fans that agents have too much power and money in the game, and such concerns have only strengthened in recent years. Few, however, would hold on to their grievances so strongly if it meant missing out on a new signing. Unfortunately the rest of football, even if they were sympathetic to the cause, didn't take up arms to support him, making Blackpool isolated in the way they did business.

Dispute after dispute came and went over the years, with companies and contracted workers complaining they weren't paid what they were owed. One person described the scene in his office, where at any point in time Karl had a stack of invoices on his desk that needed paying. It was alleged he would delay as long as possible. The ones who threatened legal action were put to the top to pay first and the others were set to one side, as he tried to win a war of attrition. Another source inside the club recalled seeing him rip up cheques that were sent to his office for signing, and said getting payment from him 'was like getting blood from a stone'. Both Karl and club financial controller Rod Dyer strongly denied this version of events, explaining he was simply protecting the business and that he took his time doing his due diligence on the thousands of payments he had to sign off on. Certainly, keeping a watchful eye over outgoings was an important part of running the club in a responsible manner; however, Blackpool gained a reputation as a business you had to think twice about getting into bed with, for fear of not getting full payment.

One of his best friends, a man called Mark Bradley, let Karl stay on his sofa on and off for two years following his divorce. Karl had been carrying on an affair with a worker in the accounts department. She eventually got pregnant and had his child, although after a dispute over money, Karl and his other children did not have a relationship with them. After his divorce, he was practically tied at the waist to Bradley, who had for years been a sponsor at the club through the local building company he owned. He was invited on official club trips, on holidays abroad, and they frequently went out drinking together in Blackpool on Saturday nights. Bradley worked on the construction of the new South Stand when it was eventually erected, but he alleged Karl didn't pay him for the materials he spent tens of thousands of pounds on, leaving him financially ruined. Karl claimed Bradley took shortcuts and didn't fully carry out sound insulation, and that others involved in the project raised their own concerns. For Bradley, it was more that Karl could not help his own nature, just as in the parable of the scorpion and the frog. After years of close friendship – Bradley was even an usher at his wedding – he alleged Karl bankrupted him.

After his early release from prison, Owen Oyston dipped in and out of the stadium offices on a whim. Karl still ran the club, but Owen enjoyed owning the team. He liked the power and influence. The players and staff knew how to humour him and work him to get what they wanted. On team nights out at restaurants, they would be ordering pizza and spaghetti, until somebody invited Owen. Then all of a sudden, they swapped to filet mignon and champagne. It was the polar opposite to Karl, who would often 'forget' his wallet when the bill came. If he did pay, he wouldn't leave a tip. Owen would have to sneakily place one on the table as they left, without him realising.

One season, after a win in the League One play-off semi-finals, the team called Owen in the middle of a celebratory night out to join them. He was quick to arrive and throw his money around. 'Oh my boys, my lads!' he would say. It was a particularly sad scene; a man in his early 70s wanting to stay out all night partying with footballers in their 20s. He went into the offices on Monday looking to hand off the £6,000 bill he had picked up. Karl refused to cover it, 'You're the one who's made the grand gesture, they knew you were going to pay!' This happened over and over again. He craved the attention.

Day to day, Karl ran the club how he saw fit without much disruption from his dad. But Owen would insert himself into issues, usually if he'd seen the manager or a staff member at the club restaurant. He would pop himself down on their table for the night with a bottle of red and promise to sort any problems they had. Karl and Owen would have raging arguments, often ending in Owen shouting 'I own the fucking club', but with Karl figuring out a method to get his own way in the end. Board meeting after board meeting became screaming matches between father and son. While others accused Karl of refusing to make payments the club owed, he made the same accusation against his father. He claims that at one point Owen had been asking the club's subcontractors to carry out work for his own external projects, and they had called Karl to complain they hadn't been paid. Karl emailed all the club's suppliers with a warning. Don't do any work for Owen Oyston. If you do, don't come moaning to the club when you don't get paid.

Whatever they were doing, for a long time it worked. Nobody could deny Blackpool's success on the pitch. Their Third Division play-off final win over Leyton Orient in 2001 was followed up with two more trips to the Millennium Stadium, as they lifted the Football League Trophy – then known as the LDV Vans Trophy – twice in three years. The club attracted foreign investment when Latvian banker Valeri Belokon bought a 20 per cent stake in 2006, putting a modest amount of money in to help take them to the next level. He came to England with the hope of flogging beer from the brewery he owned in Riga. He was looking to sell his products in English football stadiums, but he struck up a much bigger relationship with Owen. After some negotiation, he ended up part-owning the club instead. His money helped pay for key additions to new manager Simon Grayson's squad, and they were promoted again via the play-offs. This time their final heroics were at Wembley, as they finished the 2006/07 season with a perfect ten victories in a row to return to the second tier of English football for the first time in 29 years. They fought off relegation and continued to consolidate their position, despite losing Grayson to Leeds midway through their second season in the league. With improvement after improvement, some incremental, others great leaps forward, they had become an established Championship club.

After their relegation to the basement division in 2000, what followed was a decade of success unrivalled by few outside of the truly elite clubs. Two promotions, two cup wins, and a feeling that the club was going from strength to strength. A section of fans still grumbled. Some because they just enjoyed doing so, others because they were truly prescient in seeing that the foundation was built on sand. This brings us to the final season of the decade, when Blackpool achieved the unthinkable. Their promotion to the Premier League in 2010 was majestic. It was a miracle. It was the best trip thousands of fans, spanning generations, had ever been on. It set about the wheels of motion which started with delirious success, then crumbled and collapsed, as Blackpool became the most controversial and crisis-laden club in British football. This is the story of what happened next.

Chapter 1

The Best Trip

IN THE summer of 2009, Blackpool had a vacant managerial position.

The obvious choice was caretaker manager Tony Parkes, who had successfully steered the team to safety after Simon Grayson departed at Christmas. Right up until the flashing news bulletin confirmed otherwise, Grayson had been telling people he would stay. He was asking senior players to ignore interest from other clubs to help him build for the future in Blackpool. Ultimately, however, he jumped at the chance to join his boyhood club, and orchestrated the move with Leeds behind Karl Oyston's back. Oyston took the Yorkshire club to tribunal for tapping him up and won a settlement figure close to what was left on his contract. Meanwhile, Parkes picked up the pieces and led the team to an even better second half to the season than the first. With ten games left they were just one place and one point above the relegation zone, but pulled through the mini-crisis and only lost one more game the rest of the way, finishing a comfortable 16th. After all that, he declined the permanent job in the summer.

He told the club it was a decision made in tandem with his wife, to spend more time at home. When it came to telling the media, the story changed. He explained that the money offered wasn't good enough, 'I felt the offer was unjust and there was no way that I could accept it … I can't understand why I had that kind of offer after what I'd done.' Whatever the reason, the search was on for a new appointment. Alan Knill from Bury interviewed, as did ex-Huddersfield boss Andy Ritchie. Club-favourite Gary Brabin, who played for Blackpool in the late 90s, was called in but didn't impress. He had just lost in the Conference play-off final with his Cambridge team and hadn't had much time to prepare. Nobody jumped out, until they got to Ian Holloway.

'Ollie', as he was known, had spent a year out of football after being sacked at Leicester. It had been a huge opportunity, but a risky one. He jumped ship midway through the season from Plymouth, where he was adored by the fans. The gamble backfired. In his sole season in charge, Leicester were relegated and Holloway was axed. It took 364 days for him to get his next job, when he signed the contract at Blackpool. During his year out he looked inwards at himself and how he wanted to build a team, and outwards beyond Britain's shores, to the styles of football gracing the continent. Throughout his last few years as a manager he'd played a defensive style of football: 4-4-2, with solid banks of four, the wingers tracking back and covering the full-backs. All very rudimentary stuff. Where had it gotten him? Leicester had been his biggest opportunity yet, but it ended in failure. He saw a team of players who had lost interest in what made the game beautiful. Under owner Milan Mandarić, the club had thrown large contracts at players well past their primes. Some were about to retire and had little interest in pushing their body through another gruelling season, but couldn't say no to the money on the table. One player wasn't getting into the team, so Ollie lined up a loan move for him, but he refused. 'I'm going to sit here and make them pay me every single penny on my contract,' he said. They didn't want to win. They didn't want to better themselves.

Holloway started to think about a new way to approach the game. His introspection was prompted one day after talking to his best friend in football, Gary Penrice, an ex-forward who was working for a scouting agency in France. Penrice called him up and told him bluntly, in a way only close friends can do, 'Why don't you just get back to being creative like you used to be? I've watched you; your team just defends. You've got your wingers defending. Do yourself a favour. Build. Be creative.'

Watching football all over the world had opened Penrice's eyes to what was possible, and he wanted to share it. 'Ollie, England is an island, right? We can't look over at how anybody else is doing it. We can't look over the fence at our neighbour's garden. Here in France, you can nip over and see that football's just beautiful everywhere. You haven't got to play it one way. Write your own way of playing it. Make up what you want.'

The flames of inspiration started to flicker. Ollie spent hours writing ideas down, imagining how his next team would play. He had chickens in his garden and would line them up in formation and envision how the ball would move between them. He wanted to make the pitch smaller. Everything focused on shape. Each player would have it drilled into them over and over again, knowing exactly where to be at all times. Intricate passing triangles on one side of the pitch would drag opposition players out of their defensive shell where they were comfortable, and at that moment his team would hit a *switch* – a long diagonal to the opposite wing where they would have an overload, two v one against the full-back. Holloway's plan was not terribly sophisticated, but it was ahead of its time. It borrowed from other teams and put his own spin on it. He wanted to play good, attractive football – but at a time when the footballing world was copying Barcelona and tiki-taka, misunderstanding Pep Guardiola's masterpiece and getting lost in pursuit of possession over everything else, Holloway wanted to attack. He wasn't dogmatic in following some ideal of keeping the ball. It was about relentlessly striking with it and dealing the greatest damage possible. Above all else, it was about fun. He wanted to make the game fun.

He just needed a team. It was a long journey up to Blackpool and he nearly cancelled the interview, but his wife Kim pushed him to go for it. He turned up to Bloomfield Road and waited. And waited. Karl arrived late – he'd been busy interviewing other candidates. 'They're not fit to lace my boots!' Holloway declared when he heard their names. 'And why haven't you got a tie on?' he asked Karl, who had turned up in jeans and a scruffy shirt. 'I'm the chairman, I don't need to wear a tie,' Karl replied. 'Right!' Ollie hit back, taking his own tie off. He bought the coffee for the meeting, already aware of Oyston's reputation, 'I know you're too tight to pay for it,' he joked. Despite this being the best chance he'd been given in a year, Holloway wanted Karl to convince *him* to be manager. He had a list of questions and flipped the interview on its head. Top of the list, 'Why have the fans been slagging you off?' And then, 'Why haven't you built all the stands yet?'

The two got on immediately; the interview was a vision of how the next three years would go. They could say whatever they wanted to each other, what they really meant. There were no illusions, no false promises. Karl told him straight away, 'If you want something from me, you've got to prove you need it. Whatever I throw at you, you've got to be able to answer it and then I might get you it.' Holloway would get used to being told no over and over again before he got a yes. The interview lasted for four and a half hours. At the end, Karl slipped a piece of paper over the table containing his offer, and promptly left to go to the toilet. The offer was insulting, half what a manager of Holloway's stature could expect. Even after the two sides reached a compromise, Oyston threatened to call the whole deal off once Holloway's agent came calling for his ten per cent, but Ollie rang him back, livid, 'Who do you think you are talking to me like that? He's *my* agent. *I'll* pay him.' The deal was done.

The first of many major battles occurred on Holloway's first day, when he saw the team's training ground at Squires Gate. It was a miserable place consisting of pitches unfit for purpose and a series of connected portacabins masquerading as something that could loosely be described as a 'facility'. In one of his first interactions with the media, the manager called it a 'hell hole'. On the entrance, above a bin, read the sign 'Blackpool Football Club Training Ground & Centre of Excellance'. Nobody seemed to notice or care that 'excellance' was spelt wrong. Holloway's biggest concern was the pitch, with heavy divots in the turf making it unsafe for his players. He was on the phone to Karl that very morning, 'You ain't done any work to this.' He was right; the training ground was the same as it was when Stanley Matthews was running up and down it in preparation for the 1953 FA Cup Final. Karl came back down the line, 'Don't start moaning about that!' but Holloway was persistent. He forced his boss to travel to the training ground to see for himself. Perhaps it was fate. That weekend Karl had been enjoying a family party and injured his ankle playing a game of tig with his children. He came to Squires Gate on crutches. 'Go on then, walk up and down that,' Holloway challenged him. He did, and sure enough he turned his ankle again, injuring it further. Holloway bellowed from the sidelines, 'See! It's not safe for my players, it's not even safe enough for you!'

He had made his point. Karl arranged for the team to rent facilities elsewhere while work was done on the training pitches. The problem was, of course, that the facilities they rented were still far superior to even the improved Squires Gate – which Ollie and his team had to come back to. Still, it was a win. His first win. It's likely that nobody had ever gotten a concession like that from the chairman before, and it went exactly how Karl promised it would in the interview. His first, second and probably third response was 'no', but Holloway proved he needed it and managed to convince him. Further improvements were made, and Oyston sanctioned more expensive hotels for the team to stay at on away trips. The club was becoming more professional under Holloway's insistence. Less than the bare minimum was no longer accepted.

Talk turned to transfer targets. In last year's January transfer window, Blackpool had brought in Charlie Adam on loan from Rangers. He became an instant fan favourite in spite of, or maybe because of, getting a red card in his first game. He'd stamped on Richie Wellens, an ex-Pool player turned designated pantomime villain, always jeered by the crowd when he returned. Once Adam was back in the starting line-up after his suspension, he never left. Priority number one was securing his services again. As Holloway watched tapes of the previous year's games, he called Matt Williams. Williams was the club secretary, but in reality was more akin to a chief executive, just without the title or pay. 'Who is this guy, why isn't he with us now?' Holloway asked. Williams had a good relationship with Rangers. It was he who had called them the previous year to enquire about a loan deal for a different player, Alan Gow. Gow went to Norwich instead, but Rangers suggested Charlie Adam as a replacement. Their sales pitch went, 'There's this other lad, he plays on the left and he's a bit overweight, but he's got a hell of a left peg.' They brought Adam in, stuck him in the middle, and he immediately impressed. Williams told Ollie he was probably available to buy, but Karl would never stump up the cash. 'Don't tell me never,' Ollie pressed, and he gave the list of his main targets to Karl.

Karl told him he didn't want to spend on Adam. Then he said the same thing to the directors in a board meeting. The money certainly wasn't going to come from Owen Oyston's bank account; that tap had been turned off long ago. The club didn't have the spare change lying around either – they were losing money despite selling key players such as Wes Hoolahan, Kaspars Gorkšs, and Shaun Barker. In stepped minority shareholder Valeri Belokon, who was ready to inject more cash after his initial investment three years previously. Belokon talked to Holloway directly, 'Ian, why do you want this player? Why him?' Holloway was ready with a small dossier on players he'd scouted while out of the game. He flipped through them all. 'These aren't good enough, these can't do the job, I need Charlie.'

Holloway had already worked his magic on Belokon, who was initially furious with his hiring – because Karl had done it without informing him. 'Right, we have to go and see Valeri,' Karl told Ian after he signed his contract. It was the first time he'd heard his name. Belokon valued loyalty above almost everything and was disturbed that Holloway had walked out on his contract at Plymouth. They all travelled to Riga for overdue introductions. After a boozy night, Holloway couldn't sleep. He just wanted a chance to prove himself. He got up at 6am and walked to Belokon's bank offices so they could talk again, privately. Belokon was surprised to find him waiting there, impressed at both his dedication and his sense of direction to find his way in the first place. That morning they talked about life. They talked about Ollie's children, three of whom are deaf, and with great openness and honesty he shared stories of how hard he worked to build a better future for them. Belokon got a sense of what type of man he was. After Holloway showed him the players he'd bought, developed, and sold on for more money at his previous clubs, Belokon decided it was a sound investment. He decided to put his trust and his money in him.

Adam's agent also helped organise pre-season trips abroad, and was on a European tour that summer with Preston. Blackpool got wind he was steering his client towards their arch-rivals. They realised the urgency needed to secure the deal and avoid disaster. It all looked set and the fee was agreed – a new club record transfer of £500,000, nearly doubling the old one. Then, Owen Oyston decided he wanted to get involved. He always thought he could secure a better deal when one presented itself. He demanded that Matt Williams email Rangers to inform them of his new offer. Blackpool would pay nothing, but if they got promoted, Rangers would get £1m. 'I'm not doing that, Owen, it's all been agreed!' Matt balked. While time would show that the offer would have been in their favour, neither Rangers nor anybody at Blackpool, barring Ian Holloway, seriously believed they were anywhere close to even being on the cusp of promotion. They had finished 16th the year before, some 18 points away from sixth place. But Williams had to follow orders, and it didn't go well. Belokon came to the rescue, promising to pay all the money up front himself in exchange for a 70/30 split of the profits. Adam scored 19 goals that season, led the team to promotion, and etched his name forever into the history books of Blackpool FC. Once the season finished and Blackpool *had* secured their promotion, Owen Oyston sent an email to Rangers, letting them know he'd been right all along. They should have taken his offer.

With the squad largely in place, it was time for Holloway to meet the players and sell them on how they were going to play. They learnt the 4-3-3 system and shape he'd practised with his chickens. He was burning with a passion to develop players, to improve them. He asked them, was Lionel Messi *born* with a ball at his feet, or was he *made*? Holloway didn't believe in God-given talent. You worked for every little thing you got, and he only wanted those who would work. They were the values instilled in him by his late father. 'He worked in die-casting – steaming hot, molten metal. He was a milkman; he was a labourer. He worked his ass off basically, for fuck all. We were in a council house when he died. He died worrying that he hadn't kept up with the insurance, so mum and us wouldn't have anything.'

A youngster called Ishmel Demontagnac joined the team and quickly showed his ability, including scoring a brace in a dominant individual performance in an early cup game against Premier League outfit Wigan. Holloway had Demontagnac spend his first four weeks running up and down the side of the training ground. The squad as a whole did much less fitness work in the pre-season than they were used to, focusing more on sessions working with the ball. But Holloway wouldn't let Demontagnac join in until he proved his fitness. Until he proved that he wanted to work. That was the attitude the rest of Blackpool's squad had and demanded of each other. It was a tight-knit group too. The nucleus of the team had been together for several years. They just needed someone to take them to the next level.

Blackpool fans took to Holloway early. It was love at first sight. He loved the quirkiness of the people and the town, and they loved the way he talked them up. Whereas Karl Oyston continually went out of his way to lower expectations, chastising hope and ambition as dangerous gambling, here was a manager not just promising Blackpool could be great, but expecting it. He knew how to play the media game, conducting early press conferences from his usual table at a local café over a cup of tea and a bacon butty. During a TV interview at the training ground, a couple of fans noticed the windows behind him had broken glass following a break-in, so they turned up the next day to install new ones. In return they asked the club for two season tickets, valued well below the cost they could have charged for installing the large, armoured windows. Karl refused. They were happy to do the work anyway.

Brick by brick, they were building something new. Holloway, the players and the people all came together in support of one another. They created the spirit Ollie needed to keep confidence in the team high. If they went 1-0 up the fans were singing and the drum was banging. If they went 1-0 down, the fans sang just as loud and the drummer smashed away regardless, roaring the players on. Holloway looked at the pictures adorning the walls at Bloomfield Road of club legends like Stanley Matthews and Stan Mortensen. He told the players, 'This group of supporters, I want them to think of you that way in 40 or 50 years. Why can't you be famous? Why can't you do something special? Why has it got to be them all the time?'

At the first pre-season friendly, the players were buzzing after receiving their bonus pay for earning survival the previous season. Holloway went into a rage, shouting at them, 'Why are you talking about that?' He went to the whiteboard and wrote '5,000,000', telling them, 'That's what I want you to get.' Team bonuses were a sore subject among the team. Unlike most clubs, Karl didn't give his players win bonuses. Instead, he offered a massive promotion bonus of £5m to be shared out collectively, based on a suggestion offered in a board meeting by Valeri Belokon. When Holloway brought it up, there were some groans. It had never been considered as an actual target. Now, he wanted it to be.

The season couldn't come quick enough. But when it did, things started off slow. Blackpool drew their first four games. Despite wanting to attack and entertain, they didn't have much to offer up top. Holloway would have to wait until the January transfer window for the reinforcements which would really up his firepower. It didn't matter, as Blackpool started to take flight anyway. After their first loss of the season six games in, away at Holloway's old team

Leicester, the 'Pool won three on the bounce. They hosted a truly memorable night at Bloomfield Road when they beat newly relegated Newcastle 2-1. The fans left the stadium practically skipping out of the exits in disbelief. They followed that up with a win away at Nottingham Forest. These results gave the players and supporters confidence that something had clicked. Holloway was right. They had something special.

They bounced in and out of the play-offs for the following few weeks, continuing to pick up points and jostling with several teams for position. In November, they beat Scunthorpe 4-1 in their last game before a break for international fixtures. It had been a goalless deadlock at half-time. 'The first half was a non-event. Quite frankly it bored me. I did not like it,' Holloway remarked after the match. Then, as so often they came to do, Blackpool were able to launch forward with attack after attack, earning themselves a flurry of second-half goals. In training, the players often ran attack drills against no defence, working on pace and passing patterns. Wave after wave of groups – *attack attack attack*. Now it was as if they were repeating the drill on matchdays. The fans were mesmerised. They went into the two-week break sitting in the play-offs, 17 games in and with everyone now daring to dream of promotion. On the coach back from matches the £5m promotion pot was all the players could talk about, and they argued over who would have the fastest sports car with their winnings.

Holloway was keeping even-keeled. He had a constant awareness of his own public persona and how he came across. He was eccentric and funny, which served him well booking TV gigs when he was out of work. Journalists knew he would always give them a good quote in a press conference; his quips became known as 'Ollieisms'. But he also found himself having to defend his 'oddball' techniques of man-management. Stories like when he cancelled training because he'd spent four hours giving motivational sermons and ran out of time, or when he walked through the team line-up with 22 charity teddy bears he'd bought the night before at his local pub, earned him plaudits for being relaxed and personable. But they were received well because Blackpool were doing well. If they were struggling, they would have told a different story.

Above all else, he wanted to be recognised as a serious football manager. He didn't want his persona to betray the number of hours he put in behind the scenes trying to improve his team. This inner tension brought a push and pull which was never too far away from breaking through to the surface. It finally did late in the season, away at West Bromwich Albion. It was Holloway's birthday the night before, and his wife Kim had travelled down with him for the game. As everyone arrived at the stadium, Kim went into a hospitality room, where the match officials were having a pre-match cup of tea. Not knowing who she was, referee Jon Moss remarked to his fourth official, 'You might have your work cut out for you today with Holloway, I hope you've brought your ear protectors.' Kim immediately called Ollie to report what she had overheard, and Ollie went ballistic. 'We're not playing the game!' he shouted to Matt Williams. 'These officials are supposed to be like jurors and he thinks I'm a clown, he thinks I'm a fucking performing seal on the touchline!' Everything stopped. Holloway told his kit man to stop unloading their gear off the bus, and 40 minutes before kick-off the team were still sat in the dressing room in their tracksuits. Williams was on the phone to the Football

League, exasperated, 'He says he's not playing!' Whether it was all performative, or if someone managed to talk him down, eventually Holloway got the team out in time for the start of the game.

For 78 minutes it looked as if everything was going smoothly. Then, as of course it was always going to happen, with the scoreline at 2-2, Blackpool defender Joe Martin brought down an attacker just outside the penalty area. Or, just *inside* the penalty area, as Moss saw it when he blew the whistle for a penalty. Graham Dorrans stepped up, scored, and Blackpool lost 3-2. They were hanging on outside the play-offs, every point was precious in the promotion race and any point away at a side second in the league was a particularly good one. It was round two after the game. Holloway ripped into Moss, but somehow escaped without a charge or ban, perhaps in an admittance of guilt from the referee of his mistake. Blackpool made a formal complaint, but nothing was ever going to come of it, although somebody from the referees' association got in touch later on down the road to apologise.

Blackpool were suffering through a loss of form in the new year. With nine games left they were eight points away from sixth place, their dreams of promotion looking like just that. A captivating season seemed likely to settle with a mid-table finish. A great improvement with plenty to look back on, but falling short of the dizzying heights they had momentarily reached out to touch. Next up was a momentous game at home with the newly constructed South Stand finally open for supporters at Bloomfield Road, nearly a decade after it had been pulled down. Valeri Belokon stumped up most of the cash for the construction – £4.75m to Owen Oyston's £1m. The grand opening was ready for a home game against Crystal Palace. It was named after club legend Jimmy Armfield, who had spent his entire 17-year playing career at Blackpool, becoming the best right-back in the world and earning 43 England caps in the process.

The stand could have opened two months earlier, but Karl Oyston had been stuck in a dispute with the contractor tasked with installing fire and electrical safety equipment in the concourse underneath. He'd hoped to open early without the concourse available to the public, forgoing the wait for the installations and resulting safety certificate, a plan which wasn't given the green light. Eventually the dispute was resolved and everything was installed and ready, but the whole process added another few weeks to the opening. When opening day did arrive, it was a lovely, warm afternoon with thousands of fans cheering on in tangerine. Blackpool had lost right-back Neal Eardley to injury but Oyston sanctioned a pricey loan move for a young Irish replacement to come in from Everton. It didn't take long into his debut for Séamus Coleman to showcase his talents, and the back four grew even stronger in his presence.

Palace came to spoil the party, scoring within three minutes, which did nothing to silence the roaring Blackpool crowd. Going 2-0 up changed little either. By this point Blackpool were used to coming from behind, fighting with every belief they could outscore their opponents. They weren't able to complete the comeback on this occasion, but clawed back to battle to an entertaining 2-2 draw. It was a good result, but much more was needed in the run-in. They needed wins, and they got them. Four in a row, including a 5-1 thrashing of fellow play-off hopefuls Swansea and a thrilling 4-2 away win at Scunthorpe. The latter came in front of a packed-out away end where the Tangerines ran riot with three goals in the final 15 minutes. They went up to Newcastle and lost 4-1, but it was merely a bump in the road and they won their next two, marking six wins in seven. It was a run of form that had everybody believing if they could just get to the play-offs, they were unstoppable. A culmination of time and place, of individual and team – one of those magical periods athletes only get a few times in their short careers.

It all came down to the final game of the season, at home to Bristol City. Their run had vaulted them into sixth place, the last play-off spot. Below them were Swansea, who needed a win and Blackpool to lose or draw to jump over them. In case the league table didn't quite capture the full significance of the occasion, the atmosphere before the game at Bloomfield Road filled in the rest of the picture. It was a certain kind of nervousness and anticipation. Pre-match traditions were carried out religiously, every tiny detail pre-planned and performed to perfection in sacrifice to the gods of superstition. Fans got in their seats early. The crowd vibrated with a collective angst, surging from seat to seat, row to row. Inner turmoil was disguised by the belting out of songs of victory. Then they surrendered to the blow of the whistle. They gave over their nerves and their hopes and their dreams and in that moment all they could do was watch. Helpless spectators.

Nicky Maynard put Bristol City 1-0 up after 16 minutes. Hearts sank. Fans clung to their phones for news from Swansea, but the score remained 0-0. Blackpool equalised in the 56th minute, although that didn't change much. One goal from Swansea would doom them. But it never came. The clock ticked on. The game died down towards the end, with neither side able to get the winner.

Fans checked their phones. They looked up to the pitch and saw a stalemate, they looked down at their phones and saw the same. For every twist and turn they could have predicted and played out in their heads, somehow this hadn't been anticipated. They had pictured dramatic goals back and forth at the two stadiums, Blackpool and Swansea swapping places throughout the day in sixth position. But nothing was happening, and that somehow made the ticking clock more agonising. They checked their phones once more. Blackpool played the ball forward and delivered a cross into the box. Screams of joy were suffocated before they could begin as the goalkeeper plucked the ball out of the air and nestled it safely into his chest. Back to the phones. News began to trickle through in the stadium that Swansea's game had finished. It was over. Blackpool were in the play-offs. Blackpool. Three games away from the Premier League.

Their opponents for the semi-final were Nottingham Forest, who in many aspects still regarded themselves as a Premier League club, despite not gracing the top division for a decade. You could almost forgive some arrogance. For the home leg at Bloomfield Road, Blackpool had an attendance of 11,805. The return leg at the City Ground had 28,358 packed in. Forest's wage bill of £15m that year tripled Blackpool's. And while Blackpool had pushed the boat out with the £500,000 signing of Charlie Adam, Forest could field an entire starting XI of players they'd paid more for. What's more, they had finished nine points better off in the league table. But Blackpool backed themselves. The two sides had already met twice, and both times Blackpool ran out the victors, including a 3-1 victory at home only three weeks earlier.

The semi-final was played on the pitch over two legs of 90 minutes, not in the club accounts at the end of the season. Only one team had proven themselves in that arena. Nottingham Forest, however, seemed particularly intent on offering up more motivation anyway. In that second meeting in April, manager Billy Davies had made four changes to the starting team, swapping out his entire front line of attackers. They had secured their play-off spot the week before, so some resting was inevitable, but this was different. With the Blackpool players leaving the pitch fresh off their victory, Davies greeted them in the dugout, rubbing his hands together. 'This is brilliant for me ... I've done this so we get you in the play-offs, if we get you in the semi-final we're guaranteed to get to the final!' The Blackpool players laughed it off. But they remembered.

The first leg was a tight affair. Forest took the lead with a curling effort at the edge of the box from Chris Cohen, but Keith Southern and a Charlie Adam penalty completed the comeback and it was Blackpool who took the day 2-1. Effectively half-time, it was advantage to the Seasiders – or so you might have thought. Not for Davies, who was again ready to welcome the Blackpool players in the dugout after the game. 'Job done,' he said. 'You aren't scoring at our place, we're gonna turn you over, don't even bother showing up!' Ian Holloway came into his dressing room laughing. 'Do I need to say anything to you now?'

Before the return game at the City Ground, the players giddily passed around the match programme which had a four-page spread on 'Team Billy', detailing his army of backroom staff. At Blackpool, Holloway leant on Steve Thompson, his number two, and Phil Horner, the physio. His performance analyst was a 19-year-old on a work placement during university years at UCLan. The kit man was a taxi driver who worked part-time for £150 a week. On his airport runs he would stop off at the stadium and unload dirty kit, with his passengers waiting in the car. He had to contend with three second-hand washing machines because Karl Oyston refused to pay for an industrial washer, despite Holloway practically begging for one on his behalf. At one point Karl eventually gave in, but only when he found a used one on eBay. When it arrived, all the instructions were in German, and they were all so confused as to how to work it that they shrunk the kits. The groundsman chipped in where he could, often ferrying food cooked at the stadium over to the training ground, which didn't have such facilities. 'I'm really worried,' he would call ahead, 'I've got all these shepherd's pies and they're all leaking in the boot of my car!' Matt Williams was told by his counterpart in Nottingham that all their players had already had their suits measured, they had put the final tickets on to their own ticketing system, and they had already booked the hotel. Williams rushed off to inform Holloway, who was absolutely buzzing when he heard, shouting off about it in front of all the players.

Some of it was probably sound planning from Forest's viewpoint. There was a short turnaround after the game if things did go to plan. But Karl Oyston refused to allow Blackpool to plan anything. In the 90s they had gotten cocky in the play-offs after beating Bradford 2-0 in the first semi-final leg away from home. Back at Bloomfield Road, the programme had a section titled 'Road to Wembley', advising fans how to book their travel and tickets for the final. Manager Sam Allardyce stuck five at the back and played for a 0-0 draw, but they ended up losing 3-0 to

Chris Kamara's extremely motivated Bradford team, who used Blackpool's overconfidence and rumours of Allardyce already having his suit measured as fuel.

Seven minutes into the second leg, Davies was feeling even more pleased with himself. Rob Earnshaw got past the Blackpool back line and scored to put Forest up 1-0. The away goal rule meant that even at 2-2 on aggregate, if the result stayed the same Forest were through. But Blackpool were never short of belief that they would score. They came out in the second half and accelerated through the gears, putting on a full show of their entire attacking force. January addition DJ Campbell scored the equaliser. He'd been with the club on loan the season before, scoring goal after goal to a chorus of 'Sign the DJ! Sign the DJ! Sign the DJ!' and had been one of Holloway's main targets in the summer. Leicester wouldn't sell him, but they agreed to another loan move midway through the season. It was a major coup, and Campbell flourished in Blackpool's attack. His movement off the ball and skill when he had it completed the jigsaw. Holloway's vision was playing out right in front of him. They were *flying*.

Against the run of play, Earnshaw scored again to give Forest the lead on the day, but it was never close after that. What followed was a demolition job as Blackpool scored three goals in seven minutes. It was a riot. There was pandemonium in the away end. Ian Holloway turned to Steve Thompson in the dugout and asked him, 'How many is that now?'

DJ completed his hat-trick, linking up in an unstoppable connection with another January signing, Stephen Dobbie, borrowed from Swansea. Dobbie was a wizard with the ball at his feet in the number ten role and carved through the

Forest defence mercilessly. It was simply one of the finest displays of attacking football ever seen in a play-off game. A last-minute consolation for Forest capped off the match, and Blackpool had won 6-4 over the two legs. The players made sure to catch Davies on their way off the pitch. 'Job done! Have a nice holiday!' they shouted as they bounced down the tunnel. 'Cheer up Biiiilllly Davies!' rang out of the dressing room.

The team staff tried to buy some champagne and beer from Forest club officials, who understandably were utterly despondent from the defeat. 'Well, who's paying for it?' one asked. Karl Oyston was there but, as was custom, had forgotten his club credit card. The others had a whiparound and scraped some money together. It bought them three bottles of Prosecco and 20 bottles of Budweiser, just about one beer for each player in the matchday squad. Hardly enough to celebrate a trip to Wembley. The party needed more fuel, so the lads got changed and hopped on the team bus, stopping off at a petrol station to load up on more booze. They were all there in their Blackpool tracksuits. Greeting them at the shop were a handful of Forest fans. 'Oh no, here we go,' Steve Thompson worried, but in good grace the Forest fans laughed off the bizarre situation and clapped the players as they left, having emptied the shop of beer.

As the players took the party into Blackpool, preparation for the final began at Bloomfield Road. Much had already been done for them. Karl recoiled at the price, but Williams was able to take over everything Forest had already booked, even their hotel reservation. Then came the fight for the suits. The players were thinking Hugo Boss or some expensive bespoke tailor. 'Nope,' Karl said. 'We had Marks & Spencer suits last time we got to a final, get them again.'

A short wait followed to see who their opponents would be, with Leicester and Cardiff playing their second leg the following night. The players watched on, hoping for a Cardiff win. They felt Leicester had been something of a bogey side for them, whereas if they got Cardiff, they were promoted. It was that simple. It wasn't arrogance, it was the confidence a group of people had in themselves after the slog of a long season – 48 games down and on a roll with eight wins in their last ten. The team watched together as Cardiff triumphed over Leicester in a tense penalty shoot out. The final was all set.

They travelled down to London a few days beforehand. They were on top form in training, mixing in games of mini-golf to wind down. The morning of the final, as everyone filtered downstairs for breakfast, Ian and Kim Holloway were together on a table. 'How are you feeling, Gaffer?' someone asked. 'Great! I've had the best night's sleep ever – do you know why?' He left a pause, always nailing the comedic timing, 'Because I've been sleeping in Billy Davies's bed!' Holloway and Thompson made sure all week to always be seen relaxed and smiling, making jokes. Whatever nerves they may have felt deep down, they weren't going to let the players see them. Elsewhere, a less confident Owen Oyston was scrambling to change the agreement with Cardiff over revenue sharing. Tradition went that the winner gifted the loser full share of the gate receipts, plus a small bonus. They'd be headed to the Premier League with a £90m payday, so it was a gesture to the loser that they could at least keep all the money from the day. Never content to let a deal go untinkered with, Owen was pushing Cardiff to agree to a higher bonus for the loser, in case Blackpool were beaten.

The players were more confident, but as they arrived at the stadium the weight of the day took hold. The oppressive heat pushed down on them like a thick blanket from above. It was *sweltering*. During the game the Sky cameras routinely cut to a pitch-side thermometer, which inched ever closer to 40°C. Pre-match, the players found a pocket of shade in the corner of the pitch and did most of their warm-ups there. Back in the dressing rooms, they noticed something different. Steve Thompson's son Curtis usually helped out before games, getting the players' boots ready and all lined up under their stall. But Curtis was in the stands. 'Get him down here!' the players shouted. Someone managed to get to him, through the masses of fans already in their seats, and brought Curtis down to ease superstitions. Then all eyes turned to Holloway as he gave the biggest team talk of his life. He reflected on what was going through his mind in a recent interview. 'Enjoy the game as much as we can, make it the most entertaining play-off final ever. And then dream we were good enough at the end of it.'

Blackpool went 1-0 down just nine minutes into the game. They were going to have to pull themselves out of a hole. 'So what?' Brett Ormerod asked the rest of the team. 'Go pick the ball up, let's go and score.' Ormerod had returned to Blackpool the previous season after eight years away. At 33 years old, his game had been revitalised under Holloway. The 13 goals he scored that year were as many as he'd scored in the three previous. 'So what?' was their philosophy. Holloway's attacking values had prepared them for this moment. 'You get the principle of playing in their mind that we're gonna score the next goal, all the time. Your game plan never, ever changes. We go 1-0 up, we're gonna try and score the next goal. We go 1-0 down, so what? Our game plan's the same, we gotta try and score the next goal.'

They won a free kick, in the Cardiff half but 30 yards away from goal. Charlie Adam took the ball. A couple of other players hovered around but there was no way the captain was going to let anyone else take it. The day before, at the end of a training session, he had placed one right into the top corner from a similar position. He walked off the pitch and on to the team bus without breaking stride. 'I'll do the same tomorrow if I get the chance,' he promised. The others laughed it off; their lack of confidence arguably well placed. Adam had scored a free kick early on in the season by blasting the ball through the wall, the sheer power displacing bodies and slamming into the back of the net. It was a great goal, but for the rest of the season he failed to repeat the same success with the technique, often struggling to get past the wall. All those free kicks Charlie Adam had taken in the season, the many thousands he'd practised in training, all went out the window. It was just him, the ball, and 30 yards separating him and legend. The goal he scored was one of the greatest ever at Wembley. His celebration, floating back across the pitch towards the Blackpool fans, both arms outstretched, a single finger on each hand pointing outwards, is painted in the memory of every supporter. It is memorialised on canvas hung up in restaurants, bars and barber shops along the Fylde coast.

Blackpool grew into the game. It wasn't their best performance, but they were starting to keep more of the ball and play on their terms. Then, when it was all beginning to look comfortable, a Cardiff player slipped in front of a through ball which pierced the Blackpool defence and directed the ball past goalkeeper Matt Gilks. Blackpool had to come back, again. So what? They kept attacking, kept pushing forward, and two minutes later won a corner from a beautiful spell of football. David Vaughan took the ball and passed it to Keith Southern dropping into the number ten position. On the turn he flicked it first time to Ormerod on the edge of the box, who chested it down for Gary Taylor-Fletcher to strike on the half-volley. One-touch, quick, instinctive interplay. The shot rapped the post and fell back to the onrushing Ormerod. Triumph and disaster were separated by inches. A Cardiff defender got there first and cleared the ball out of play. Blackpool hit a high corner and the goalkeeper rushed out, but couldn't make clear contact on his attempted punch. The ball dropped and with his back to goal DJ Campbell made an audacious attempt to invent a shot, with the ball curling around his back. His shot was blocked and fell to defender Ian Evatt, also with his back to goal, who tried an even more audacious overhead kick. It was cleared off the line by a Cardiff player. Gary Taylor-Fletcher stuck his head in the inches of space between the heavy traffic of boots and bodies and squeezed the ball, finally, into the back of the net. All square, again.

Brett Ormerod hadn't slept the night before. He was a nervous wreck. Nine years previously he'd scored in Blackpool's 4-2 victory over Leyton Orient in the Third Division play-off final. It hardly compared. He spent the night staring at the ceiling. Nobody understood the importance of the occasion for the club and the fans more than Ormerod. He represented them. He was a Lancashire lad who was working in a cotton mill and playing part-time with Accrington Stanley in non-league football before he got his break at Blackpool in 1997. At Bloomfield Road, he formed one half of a devastating partnership up front, a classic big-man-little-man combination with John Murphy. When he got his next big move to Premier League Southampton, a friend gave him three booklets filled with page after page of comments printed from a fans' message board, all professing their love and wishing him the best of luck. He was hundreds of miles away from home, sat alone in a hotel room. He read those comments over and over again, for days. He kept hold of them as the years went on, eventually taking them with him back to Blackpool in the twilight of his career.

He was tired in the 46th minute. It was injury time, the half-time break seconds away. But there was one attack left. It was Vaughan again in the middle of the park with the pass that started the move, hitting Séamus Coleman on the right-hand side with a slightly lofted ball. Cutting inside, he drove forwards, dragging defenders with him. He played it into DJ Campbell, who had Cardiff players surrounding him. Somehow, he escaped, twisting and turning and getting a sight at goal. He cocked his foot back, set to unleash. Then he slipped. Then two Cardiff players slipped. Chaos and calamity befell the pitch but one thing kept moving – the ball. Rolling on as if by some mystic force placing it in the perfect place, at the perfect time, for Brett Ormerod. It was over in a flash, rushing on, prodding it through the bodies and into the goal. Inches. Triumph won. Blackpool took the lead for the first time in the game, and never let go. The song still rings around Bloomfield Road, 'Who put the 'Pool in the Premier League? Super Bretty Ormerod!'

Fans stayed behind in the stadium for what felt like hours after the final whistle. In the giant, towering stands at Wembley, they were far away from the players, but had never felt closer. As the players did laps of honour and threw champagne on each other, Steve Thompson took out his phone. It had only been ten minutes since the game ended, and in the middle of the jubilant scene playing out around him, Thompson took time to send a text message to director Gavin Steele, who years earlier had taken him from the launderette he was running and asked him to coach the youth team at Blackpool, before he was promoted to the senior side. He wrote him a simple message. 'Thank you for getting me back into football.'

That night the team met up at the Royal Gardens in Kensington, a five-star hotel with an extremely expensive drinks menu. 'You're going to have to put a free bar on for everyone,' Matt Williams said to Karl. He protested, but gave in. 'Okay, I'll put five grand down, that will buy everyone a drink.' One drink. That was his thinking, hours after winning £90m. Ten minutes later, the manager at the bar informed them that the money had run out, 'Okay, I'll put another five down,' Karl said. 'Fuck off – put 20 or 30 grand down at least!' Matt urged. Karl acquiesced and paid enough money to last until the players started getting the shots in, then they were on their own. But the players weren't the only ones getting merry, and Oyston family drama was about to entertain the rest of the guests.

Karl's heavily pregnant partner, Victoria, had gone to bed early. After Victoria went up to their room, an old flame of his turned up, claiming Karl had invited her. The two were seen chatting at the bar. His daughter, Josie, also noticed the reunion and took offence. The other woman was a lot younger than her dad, closer to her age in fact. They had gotten into an altercation once before on a night out, before getting separated. At the hotel it was round two, in an ugly, hair-pulling type of wrestling fight where both ended up on the floor, glass smashing everywhere in the mess, but with no real blows landed or damage done. After it got broken up, Josie was carted away by quick-thinking friends and hidden in a room upstairs. The police arrived an hour later. They were unable to find Josie but did find Karl's 16-year-old son Sam, sat in the lobby. The girl had accused Sam of being involved, so the police arrested him, and he spent the night of Blackpool FC's promotion to the Premier League at Notting Hill police station. He needed a guardian to arrange his release but could only get through to his future step-mum, nearly nine months pregnant, to come and bail him out. He was eventually let off as CCTV footage showed he was not part of the altercation. The charges against Josie were also dropped after she came in for a voluntary interview. The police acknowledged it was a typical drunken scuffle that neither side had instigated over the other.

Back in Blackpool, 60,000 fans arrived on the pier to welcome home their heroes in an open-top bus parade. The sea of tangerine shirts reassured each person that they had not dreamt it, others had seen it too. Blackpool really were in the Premier League. 'Where have *you* been all season?!' Holloway shouted down the microphone.

Chapter 2

A Year in the Sun

THE EXCITEMENT could barely be contained. F5 keys on computers across Blackpool were worn down by the constant refreshing of message boards and news sites in hope of unearthing a rumour of a new signing. It was as if a whole new world had been discovered. They were one of a sacred, select 20 teams in the biggest and greatest league on the planet. That's what everyone kept telling them. The commodification of hype was in full swing by 2010. Deadline day itself was now a date to be circled on the calendar for football fans everywhere, with the same anticipation as a cup final.

Inside Bloomfield Road, nothing had gotten off the ground. They were already behind schedule due to the extra two weeks of play-off football cutting into their close season. There was also a small revolt inside Bloomfield Road that Karl Oyston had to deal with. Charlie Adam was taking the club to court over bonus pay. His contract stipulated that as soon as Blackpool were mathematically safe from relegation in the Championship, he was owed £25,000. But the Oystons wouldn't pay. Karl argued that the bonus was there to reward the players for staying in the league, but, after all, they hadn't stayed in the league. It was a pathetic attempt to save an insignificant sum for no real reason, alienating the team's best player and captain because they played *too* well. In a taste of things to come, the Oystons lost the case in court and Adam was awarded his money. He ended up losing more than he gained through lawyer and court fees, but it was the principle of the matter which drove him. Despite the result, Karl refused to pay out others in the squad who had similar bonus clauses, including manager Ian Holloway. Instead, he challenged them to sue him to get it. Holloway magnanimously admitted defeat, 'I always had a dream that someone would get £100m and they would want to share it out to the people who helped them get it. But over wording he tried to save himself on that and I don't blame him. I should have … we should have all had it worded much better.'

It was a violent crash back down to earth for the players who had been plotting how they would spend their slice of the £5m promotion bonus kitty, which took months to arrive. Instead, immediately after winning the biggest game of their lives, they were put on minimum wage. The paltry £90-a-week contracts in the summer weren't going to change just because they were in the Premier League. At least one player actually got a pay *decrease* upon promotion. Rob Edwards had been a regular name on the team sheet at the start of the year, but had lost his place after a couple of suspensions and a nasty cut kept him out of action. He ended the season just shy of playing enough minutes to trigger an automatic contract extension for a further year. Out of contract, he had to negotiate new terms. He'd played almost half the games and was a big voice in the dressing room. Even stuck to the bench, he continued to train hard and pushed those in front of him to up their level of play. All that counted for nothing when it came to the chairman's office. Hitting his extension would have doubled his salary, instead he was given a significant pay cut.

Three days before the first game of the season, Blackpool hadn't signed a single player. It was a source of amusement, even a warped sense of pride, for Karl Oyston. He'd laugh and point at the rolling ticker on Sky Sports News to Holloway, which read 'Blackpool Transfers In: 0.' He got such a kick out of it he took a photo and made it his phone screensaver. The club ran into an issue of money. They didn't have any, not yet anyway. The oft repeated '£90m' was talked about as if it would be delivered in a brown paper bag the day after promotion, but the truth was Blackpool would only receive half that in the 2010/11 season, staggered in instalments. The first tranche of £13m didn't arrive until August, days before the first game. The only additional revenue coming in over the summer was from boosted season ticket sales. Almost all transfers that went through required a payment up front, usually somewhere between 25 and 50 per cent. Then came added VAT and the Premier League levy to pay on top of any fee, which added another 22.5 per cent. They didn't have that money at hand.

This was the excuse Karl gave for the lack of movement. What the rest of the world didn't know yet was behind the scenes, Owen Oyston was already planning to siphon off millions of pounds from the first tranche. The day after that fateful match at Wembley, with thousands of Blackpool fans nursing sore heads from hangovers and sore bodies from the burning sun, the Oystons had pound signs in their eyes. A guest of theirs at the hotel recalled the scene in the morning as they were having breakfast. They had already circled a date in the calendar for when the first instalment would come in.

That night, Owen and Karl met with minority investor Valeri Belokon at a hotel in London. Twenty-four hours had passed since the final whistle. The street cleaners had finished cleaning up the trail of tangerine leaving Wembley and the spoils of victory had to be divided. At the Dorchester Hotel, Karl told the shareholders they should sell. The club was never going to be more valuable; now was the time to take the profits and walk away. But selling wasn't on the agenda, how could it be? Nobody gets to the top of Mount Everest just to go back down again without taking in the view. Owen suggested to Belokon that they both take some money from the club. The minutes taken recorded this figure as £3m to £5m each. In the first act of deceit against his minority shareholder, with many more to come, Owen added a little extra for himself in his own notes, 'I would like a minimum of £5m and maybe a couple of million more.' It was an informal suggestion offered presumably over many glasses of red wine and cigars, but Belokon made it clear this was the time to be spending money, not taking it out. Blackpool needed to flex their new financial muscle; dividends could wait. But, as Owen wrote in his notes, he wanted some cash so he could 'buy a few things'. To the chagrin of Blackpool fans, these 'few things' were not new players, or a new training ground. In the words of Normunds Malnacs, a director at the club representing Valeri Belokon, 'It was strange to me. You just won, everyone is in ecstasy, and they start counting money and talking how to get this money out of the club.'

A friend of Karl Oyston recalled talking to him enthusiastically about players they might sign that summer.

Instead, Karl was more excited about the interest the money would generate in the bank and through investments. 'You've got to spend some money!' his friend cried. Karl batted away concerns. The club could make do on loan deals and small transfers as they usually did. Even if they wanted to spend in the market, their lack of a recruitment network put them at a huge disadvantage. The staff hadn't been preparing for promotion; it had come from nowhere. Teams such as Nottingham Forest and Cardiff, who they had vanquished in the play-offs, would have been working in advance, identifying targets for if they went up and targets for if they didn't. Blackpool didn't have any of that. They didn't have dedicated scouts out abroad, or even much by way of domestic scouting. Holloway relied on tips from his friend Gary Penrice, or from agents touting their players with DVDs of highlights.

Holloway was expressing some concern that summer at how the club was being run, but it was mostly at his own contract. He had a one-year rolling deal, meaning at any one time he had exactly 12 months left. He came into training one day, spouting off. 'Guess how much time I have left on my deal – one year!' he shouted. Then half an hour later he said again, 'and guess how much time I have now – still a year!' He told the *Blackpool Gazette* it was a dead-end contract. It was his biggest frustration. But mostly, he was just happy to be a Premier League manager. He was practically bouncing off the walls with excitement. There were thousands of coaches in the English game, but only 20 could be in charge at the top level. For the first time, he was one of them. Any worries he did have paled in comparison to the utter joy he felt at his achievement, and his belief in what the future could hold.

Throughout his tenure, Holloway received criticism for his 'scattergun' approach in the transfer market. Even the previous year's best signings brought back loan players they already had before he came. But that summer, he did identify several targets who would have played important roles in the first team, had they secured their services. He wanted Àngel Rangel, a full-back who was a regular at Swansea. He also asked for Scott Sinclair, who he'd had on loan twice earlier in his career. Both were knocked back by Karl over money, even though they were well within the expected parameters of the sorts of players they should have been hoping to sign. It was reported that strikers Jon Stead and Brett Pitman turned down Blackpool, spurning a chance at Premier League football to join Championship side Bristol City.

Holloway did manage to line up a deal for a young centre-back from French side Clermont, Medhi Benatia. He'd been informed by Penrice that he was an upcoming free agent, and Holloway had to – *just had to* – fly over and see him in person. He did, spending a nervy flight in icy conditions before skidding down on the continent. After watching Benatia play once, he was convinced. He was desperate for a footballing centre-back who had a bit of pace to play in a high line and could bring the ball out and break through the lines. Udinese were interested, but his agent wanted him to sign with Blackpool. It was Premier League football and a style of play where he would shine, before inevitably moving on to a bigger club. Penrice told Ollie that if they moved quick, they could get him. They had a fee agreed, a modest £100,000. But Udinese offered him a four-year contract. Karl Oyston refused to offer anything better than a one-year deal, with a club option for a second.

He wouldn't compromise. Benatia went to Udinese and was later sold to Bayern Munich for £21m, and Blackpool missed out on a potential 21,000 per cent return on their investment. Five years later, when Benatia scored in the Champions League semi-final against Juventus, Ollie called up Karl Oyston from his home. 'Guess who's just blooming scored in the Champions League then!' 'Who?' came the reply. Karl wasn't watching.

At the 11th hour Blackpool were able to push some transfers through the door. Chris Basham and Craig Cathcart joined, and both carved out long Premier League careers after their stop at Blackpool. Ludovic Sylvestre became something of a cult figure among the supporters, but shone more so in future seasons when places in the middle of midfield opened up. Marlon Harewood added experience up top. All were made the week of the opening game. Inexcusably, Holloway's main priority of the summer had to wait until deadline day. Loan signing DJ Campbell, who had been so important in promotion, scoring a hat-trick in the second leg at Nottingham Forest, was desperate to make the move permanent. As was Holloway. As were the fans. It was a no-brainer. But Karl quibbled over the fee with Leicester and only made the deal at the last second, meaning he missed the first month of the season.

Fellow loanee Stephen Dobbie, who had torn the Championship to pieces in a Blackpool shirt, didn't come back. More understandable was not being able to make another deal for Séamus Coleman, who had shown so much talent in his brief stint that he forced himself into David Moyes's plans for Everton's first team. With the pair not returning, Blackpool were arguably a weaker side on paper than they were when winning promotion. It's hard to think of any other promoted team who faced the same proposition. Holloway was limited by the unofficial £10,000 weekly wage cap for new signings Karl Oyston had set. In the end, their wage bill for the year was £12.1m, dwarfed by even the next lowest in the league. They spent £3.5m on transfer fees.

Fans clamoured for the club to be more ambitious. They had reached the Premier League for the first time and might never get another chance. The investment never came, but by the end of the window they had at least done some good business. DJ Campbell returning was vital, it just took too long. Basham, Cathcart, and fellow signings Matt Phillips and Elliot Grandin were all under the age of 22. The blueprint was there to find players that could be resold in the future for higher profits. In fact, the story broke during the season that Holloway did indeed have a clause in his contract that entitled him to a percentage, which caused some consternation from fans over the possibility of a conflict of interest. They needn't have worried, as Holloway accused Karl Oyston of refusing to pay out. He claimed he never got a single penny from sales, although this was at odds with Oyston's recollection, as he contended he did receive some figure.

The injection of youth was promising, but the club struggled to sign players in the 27–32 age range who were ready to contribute right away. To reduce the talent gap on the rest of the league they needed more players at the peak of their careers. Instead, the onus mostly fell on the players who had already overachieved so much at a lower level. They had been pencilled in as relegation favourites in the Championship season, but defied all expectations with their heroics to win promotion. Now, they were tasked with overachieving on an even bigger scale.

As the pre-season went on it became evident the money was not going to be spent on the playing side of the club. There was hope and speculation that it would at least go to the right areas behind the scenes. Perhaps the board weren't going to throw money at the squad, but instead would invest in building a structure whereby they could compete in the long term. They needed to hire scouts to put together a recruitment network. They needed to build a new training ground to finally put Squires Gate out of its misery. They could put more resources behind new, modern departments such as analytics and sports science. None of that happened. It would be revealed in the following years just how much money the Oystons pocketed for themselves, but at the time all Blackpool fans could do was hope one day the changes would come. Holloway reflected back on the missed opportunity. 'What did we get out of it? We got some new popup sprinklers, that's all we got. My legacy wasn't a new training ground, it wasn't a better team once we finished.'

In preparation for the new season, a delegation of Premier League officials came down to Bloomfield Road to introduce themselves and take a look around. They met with Karl Oyston and Matt Williams, and also asked to meet with the head of commercial, head of media, head of facilities and other department heads. Karl looked at Williams and said, 'Well, those are all him – if you need me give me a shout!' and left, leaving an embarrassed Williams to conduct the tour and explain Blackpool's unique way of doing things himself. Later came the Premier League AGM weekend. The first night was a formal dinner where the chairmen met together to welcome the newly promoted teams. It was the sort of occasion where the tables are full of wine bottles and pint glasses are never empty. Karl got very drunk. Whether it was the nerves of the occasion, rubbing shoulders with the football elites, or the fact he couldn't handle his booze, he was out of control. Seeing Bolton chairman Phil Gartside from across the room, he shouted, 'Oi Garty, us being promoted – fucked your Premier League right up hasn't it!' Some of the other Blackpool staff ushered Karl away, and he sat down next to Darren Eales from West Brom. 'Where are you from then?' Karl asked. 'I'm West Brom, Karl, I'm Jeremy Peace's right-hand man.' (Jeremy Peace being the chairman and owner.) 'Fucking Jeremy Peace!' Karl went off. 'What a cunt ... anally searches you anytime you don't have a tie on.'

The annual dinner usually went on until 4am, but by 2am the room had emptied. 'Well, we've seen them all off!' Karl roared. He was gaining a reputation for his antics. It was claimed that at other such formal dos he would get drunk and lob sweets and sugar cubes around, taking aim at nearby tables which had directors or chairmen on from clubs he didn't like. Allegedly, things turned violent on one occasion, when Karl got into an altercation with an official from a lower-league club. Both men were apparently beyond drunk and the other was being rude, but Karl is said to have escalated things physically. The event was more than a decade ago and stories change from person to person, but one witness said it was pushing and shoving, another said he saw Karl punch him and he fell to the floor before it fizzled out. Karl denied this ever occurred.

More harmlessly, he'd shown himself up in similar fashion at a game against Crystal Palace, owned by another eccentric, Simon Jordan. Jordan made everyone wear ties and wouldn't allow guests to drink out of bottles. Karl and a friend ended up pissed, drinking bottles of Beck's with their ties wrapped around their head *Rambo*-style. There was a lot of talk throughout the year about how the Premier League didn't like Blackpool. It was a chip on the shoulder that Holloway used throughout his press conferences as a motivational tactic. The underdog card was one of the few they had to play. But if it was true, it might have had more to do with Karl's behaviour, than anything else to do with the team.

After some early fitness work, it was time for the team to get some games under their belt. The players hoped for a tour abroad. A warm weather camp in Spain or Portugal, maybe even Dubai. Instead, they were sent to play in a tournament in Devon, on the recommendation of Holloway. He wanted to take his team down to the southwest, where he hailed from. It was a near ten-hour coach journey from Blackpool and they arrived late. They kicked off their first game 45 minutes after getting off a cramped bus, where they had been sitting down all day. If that was asking for an injury, the state of the playing surface – a local cricket club pitch – was practically begging for one. During a game, forward Billy Clarke came down awkwardly on his ankle and that was it, the season was over for him before it started. League Two team Wycombe refused to play their game because of the conditions. Blackpool soldiered on under Holloway's insistence.

One day at training someone turned up in boots, claiming he had a trial. None of the players knew who he was or had ever heard his name, but some had a nagging feeling they recognised him from somewhere. Not long into the session they were even more confused. He clearly wasn't a professional and had no business being on the pitch, although he was flying into challenges and getting stuck in. That night they went out for an evening meal at a local restaurant. As they sat down at their table, the same person came over with menus in hand to serve them for the evening. He was a waiter, and he'd mentioned to Holloway the night before that he used to play for a local team. So, Ollie invited him to join in training to make the numbers up.

It had been a lesson in everything that could go wrong in a summer. The calendar moved on and the words of all the sceptics in the media were still ringing through the dressing room at Wigan, as the Blackpool players got prepared for the first game of the season. 'They won't get ten points.' 'They won't even win a corner.' Nobody had predicted anything but a miserable campaign, finishing dead last with weekly drubbings on the menu. Then, Blackpool shut everyone up and shook the football landscape. They didn't just win, they demolished Wigan, in front of a jubilant travelling contingent that packed the away end and never stopped singing. It was comical, it was sublime. They won 4-0, and 4-0 looked kind to their opponents. After the game, Sky's flagship show *Soccer Saturday* featured the league table up on the screen. 'Shall we just leave it there for a moment or two?' host Jeff Stelling asked. 'Blackpool fans, you can just savour it;' 116 days after their win at Wembley, Blackpool were laying down another piece of history. They were top of the Premier League.

Adrenaline and belief brought them there and it never wavered, not even after they were hammered 6-0 at Arsenal the following week. It was the sort of scoreline writers up and down the country had been licking their lips waiting for. But they bounced back with a draw against Fulham and a win at Newcastle. They were fourth in the table. The Fulham match was their first home game of the season, bizarrely the only one in front of their own fans in the first five. They had been forced to reschedule some fixtures due to ongoing construction work at Bloomfield Road. The temporary open-air golf stand they used for away fans wasn't fit for purpose, so the club decided they should build a new stand to boost capacity and capitalise on getting more people in the ground. They had a little over three months and could only get it ready a couple of weeks into the season. Karl Oyston described it as a near miracle they even managed to get it up in that time. It was an improvement, but the new stand was still stripped back by most standards. There was no concourse underneath for toilets and refreshments, and unfortunate clusters of fans had their views obscured by the pillars holding up the roof. Still, Blackpool finally had four stands. Proper stands. With roofs. It was something of an achievement at least.

Whether it had been an impressive feat or not, the late opening was only expected to pile on the misery for Blackpool. Conventional wisdom suggested their best hope was to ride the wave of promotion to early results, but with so many away games they may have ruined their chances of even getting that. That they managed to get through the patch with so many points was a testament to the manager and players.

During the planning phase Karl decided to extend an extra half block on to either end of the stand, seemingly ignoring warnings that the extension would require new wind load tests. As predicted, the structure was declared unstable due to the wind load, so they had to knock through the back at the top of the stand to allow the wind to pass through safely. Just two and a half years after it had been open, the council held an investigation into its safety after a visiting Cardiff fan fell through the boarding he was stood on. Karl defended the stand and swatted away any criticism as only existing with the benefit of perfect hindsight. 'We had CCTV footage of them from the minute they arrived, holding on to the barrier and jumping up and down, 3 or 4 fat fans. Eventually one managed to get himself through a board. You know, if any of us went and did something ridiculous we'd probably manage to get through something pretty safe wouldn't we? We had it on video … these stupid bastards look at them! Eventually one got through.' The difference between Blackpool's stand and almost every other stand in the country was the away fans were bouncing up and down on plywood, and the club had to fix it up to make it more durable after the incident.

Even that first home game of the Premier League season against Fulham nearly fell through. Karl had hired a firm to do some work at the ticket gates, which were being upgraded to have automatic scanners. Karl and the company fell out in one of the many disputes that seemed to befall the club. Oyston accused them of using the wrong material, which was prone to rusting. The other side claimed they had been wrongly unpaid. Whatever the truth, the night before the game, someone got into Bloomfield Road and sabotaged the new scanners. In the morning, the ground officer realised the ticket gates weren't working. It was their first Premier League game and fans couldn't even get into the stands. There weren't enough people to work on all the gates to switch to a manual system. In the end, a club electrician was able to come in and fix it all in time, and the match went ahead with nobody noticing.

Back-to-back defeats to Chelsea and Blackburn were next. The game away at Stamford Bridge was a particular reminder of the gulf between the rest of the league and Blackpool. Beforehand, scout Billy Dearden had provided an opposition report which consisted of Chelsea's team sheet from the previous week and a note which read 'all the fucking best!' They went 4-0 down after 41 minutes. They didn't play particularly badly, but were simply outclassed by the talent on the pitch. It was something they had to get used to. Sometimes it didn't matter how well they were doing; they were facing players who could make something out of nothing in the blink of an eye.

After the game, Karl refused to pay for post-match dinner at £15 a head at the stadium. Instead, a staff member had to rush around a local Sainsbury's to get microwave meals for the players to eat on the coach back. That was a common occurrence. To the cameras, Holloway was gushing about the managers he was now competing with – Sir Alex Ferguson, Harry Redknapp, Arsène Wenger – he wanted to emulate the professionalism and dedication they had in their set-up. Meanwhile, his players were living off microwave meals. The Oystons didn't even want to give the players bottled water. One day during the season Karl noticed the number of bottles and sandwiches on the team coach. 'What's all this?' he exploded. 'It's fucking ridiculous, all this money!' Even Owen Oyston got involved, 'They'll just have to refill their bottles out of the tap, like I do,' he said, batting away the health concerns over reusing the same plastic bottle.

It was again down to the lower-level staff to figure out a way around the cheapness of the Oystons. One found a creative way around an expense report in order to hide the cost of the water. Other clubs had a professional chef at the training ground, supplying healthy and nutritious meals for all the players. Blackpool relied on their groundsman putting on porridge from time to time when he had the chance. McDonald's the night before a game was the norm. Chinese takeaway and Domino's pizza menus were handed out in the dressing room after post-match team talks. Players brought in from Spain or France couldn't believe their luck when full English breakfasts were put in front of them. 'Their eyes lit up like they'd won six numbers on the lottery!' assistant manager Steve Thompson joked.

They were out of their depth and had no right to be playing so well. It defied all logic. There was a near frenzy after they beat Liverpool 2-1 at Anfield, in one of their best performances of the season. The media waxed lyrical over their style of play, which was breathing new air into a league which for some reason – despite all the hype and glamour – often felt in need of such. They received a standing ovation from all corners of the stadium. Liverpool fans were staying in after the full-time whistle to protest the ownership of Hicks and Gillett, and graciously applauded the victors. After that was an international break, a chance to take stock, rest up, and maybe allow themselves to dare to look at the league table that had them sitting in ninth. Instead, they were put on a plane for a diplomatic trip.

By now the men in tangerine were not only the talk of England, but of Latvia too. Club president Valeri Belokon wanted to show off his team to his friends and business partners, so he paid for the entire squad to fly to Riga. If anyone was wondering whether Blackpool had changed with the times, whether the club had become more professional and organised behind the scenes, the trip soon proved otherwise. In a scene reminiscent of the supposedly fictional comedy film *Mike Bassett: England Manager*, they arrived at an open training session at a stadium in Riga without any footballs. 'I thought you brought them?' Holloway said to one of Belokon's men. 'No, I thought you did?' he replied. They travelled all that way for what turned into an impromptu fitness session.

Their trips to Riga were legendary, often amounting to little more than a pissed-up weekend expedition. On one such trip, several sources confirmed Karl spent the night in jail after trying to run out on an exorbitant bill some bouncers were forcing him to pay. Belokon arrived to bail him out. He felt embarrassed that his guest had been targeted as a tourist, but it wasn't the only time Karl was supposedly arrested. Sources also confirmed he had spent a night in cells back home after fighting with Blackpool fans as he left a club on a night out, punching one to the floor, leaving him bleeding and requiring stitches. There were no charges brought, and the two lads he got involved with were no strangers to drunken dustups. When put to him he flatly denied any such incident occurred, before admitting after further questioning that he had fought with the fans, that they did end up in Blackpool Victoria Hospital, but they had instigated it.

In early September, news hit that youth team coach Gary Parkinson had suffered a stroke. Parkinson had briefly played for the club in 2001 and later became head of youth development in 2006. He was a beloved member of the Blackpool family, close with many of the players and especially Steve Thompson, who Parkinson had replaced in the youth team when he was moved up to the senior squad. The stroke had a devastating impact on Parkinson.

He was rushed into intensive care and placed into a medically induced coma. He was in such a dire position that he was read his last rites twice. That he survived was a miracle, but when he was woken up doctors realised he had locked-in syndrome and was unable to move anything but his eyes.

The first game after the incident was Newcastle away, which Blackpool won 2-0. When captain Charlie Adam scored, he ran all the way to the dugout to pick up a shirt from the kit man that had '4 Parky' written on it in marker pen. Ian Evatt lifted up his shirt at the end of the game to show the same message. They held it to the cameras and the Blackpool fans high in the away stand. The players had been there to support the youth team when they were informed of the news. Young lads were bursting into tears, so a senior player would grab them, put their arm around them and take them for a little walk. Parkinson spent the next two years in hospital as his wife Debbie faced the enormous financial burden of having to redesign and renovate their home to suit his medical needs. Immediately, the call for help was answered by the football community. He had also played for Burnley, Middlesbrough, Bolton and Preston. Each club did something – a dinner, a charity event, some sort of fundraiser to help.

Gavin Steele, a director at Blackpool, set about organising their own efforts. There was already an upcoming dinner arranged to raise money for the community, and Steele proposed that 50% go to Parkinson. Staff members offered to chip in for free. The catering and cleaning were all going to be done voluntarily, so as much money as possible could go towards the Parkinson family. Then Karl Oyston got wind of it. 'I don't see why we should be doing this,' he blasted Steele, 'I've got a lad in my catering department who has cancer, we're not doing anything for him!' Gavin replied, 'Karl, this lad has cancer which is 95 per cent curable, he's still working while he does his chemo, Gary Parkinson has locked-in syndrome, he can't even move.' Just a couple of days before the dinner was due to go ahead, Karl demanded for it to be cancelled.

Karl took offence to what he termed 'grand gestures', saying, 'There was a lot of outpouring from fans about let's make these big emotional gestures, where I try to be a bit more reasonable with it.' He questioned why money was being raised for an ex-footballer, when nobody would do the same for a painter or a cleaner who worked at the club if they needed it. When asked why it had to be one or the other, why he as chairman couldn't give charitable donations to other workers from the club, he defended himself by saying 'it's not my role'. He didn't believe Parkinson, who had only played for the club in a short spell towards the end of his playing career, had developed enough status to be given such treatment. That he had run the youth team for four years wasn't seen as enough either. 'He'd not been there ten minutes compared to a lot of other people, and he played 20 odd games for us. He wasn't quite in the category as Jimmy Armfield let's say, who we'd have done anything for,' Karl said. Thankfully, after the protests of his staff, he eventually gave in on the day of the dinner and gave permission for it to go ahead, just hours before it had been scheduled.

When Karl got something in his head, he was almost blinded by everything else. He was adamant that the PFA should give Parkinson all the financial support he needed. They were the union he'd been a member of all his career. He decided to make a stand, for whatever misguided principle he felt he had. At the end of the season, a contractor suggested that the annual football game contractors played against staff at the club be made into a fun day, with money going to Parkinson's family. This time, he said, Oyston flatly refused.

Everywhere around him people were pitching in, trying to do what they could to help. At every turn, Karl tried to frustrate their support. Those inside the club were shocked at what they saw as a display of incomprehensible cruelness. Despite backlash from the PFA, Karl put Parkinson on to the statutory sick pay scheme. It was worth a paltry £79 per week, and he gave no enhancements from the club. The players had voted to donate £5k to Parkinson through their wages, but Karl received more criticism for being slow processing the payment. Even that figure Karl paid as backdated salary rather than as an ex-gratia payment, which could have been paid tax-free. Parkinson's annual wages were barely sufficient in the first place; Karl had been cutting the pay every time a new person took the job. It started at £25,000 per year, then he dropped it to £22,000 when Steve Thompson took over. When Parkinson replaced him, he cut it again to £20,000.

More than a decade on, Parkinson is still in the same condition, unable to move anything but his eyes. Steve Thompson tells the unfortunate story of the lack of support that came from the top at the club, 'You had a staff member who was struggling for money. You see every other club – Middlesbrough, Burnley, Bolton, Preston, and then Blackpool. The supporters did it, the supporters helped Parky – the club did absolutely nothing for him. Which was a massive, massive disappointment. That hurt. There's not many Blackpool staff who have even rung and asked how Gary Parkinson is. Even now, from the top level. I don't think they've had one phone call since he's been ill. That, for me, says it all. You see all these other clubs inviting him in and doing stuff for him, that's how proper clubs treat you. That's how proper people treat you. You look at how Parky got treated at Blackpool, it was absolutely horrendous.'

Karl had previously been very generous with his time and support for functions put on by the fans. He made sure to cancel other plans so he could attend tribute nights for the likes of Alan Suddick, Billy Ayre and Alan Ball, ex-players who had unfortunately passed. When the fans put on a dinner for Jimmy Armfield's 70th birthday, Karl was getting involved helping them haggle with the caterers over the cost of the meal per head. It made it even more bizarre and cruel that such generosity did not extend to a member of his own staff. He had apparently threatened to sack Parkinson on one occasion before. Parkinson was driving a 15-seater bus for the youth team at the stadium, the roads around the ground didn't all connect up at the time so he had to use a block pavement to turn around. This completely uneventful scene was playing out under Karl's nose as he looked down from his office. He had already warned players for continually using the paving, and this latest instance set him off. 'Who's fucking driving that bus?' he shouted. 'Fucking sack whoever's driving that bus!' He eventually found out it was Parkinson and got someone to tell him that he needed to write a letter of apology. Steele got wind and immediately went down to the training ground, telling Parkinson, 'You're not writing anything, you're doing nothing.' Then he came back to have it out with Karl. 'Karl, I've seen you using that pavement to turn around and I know your dad does it cause I've had to tell him off cause his car was dripping oil.' 'I'm in charge, and my dad owns the fucking club, he can do what he wants,' Karl retorted, although eventually he was talked down and the matter was settled. No doubt helped by the fact it was pointed out the land wasn't even owned by the club, but by the council.

The Christmas period brought a bitter winter cold, even for Blackpool. Whereas other stadiums had undersoil heating, Bloomfield Road was completely unequipped to deal with it. Game after game was called off. First came a night match on 4 December, at home to Manchester United. The call was made the night before to postpone due to a frozen pitch, although Blackpool were adamant that by Saturday lunchtime it would have thawed out. They suspected United were putting pressure on the league to postpone, a welcome respite as they were in the middle of an especially busy run of fixtures thanks to midweek games in the Champions League and FA Cup. Less excusable was the Boxing Day fixture at home to Liverpool, which was also postponed due to a frozen pitch. Staff were trying to get Karl to pay for overhead pitch heaters, equipment many teams even outside the Premier League had. Never one to miss a trick which would save him a few quid, Karl thought of a better idea. On Christmas Eve, he brought down some industrial heaters that blew hot air and grabbed a load of pipes to connect it all together. Then he laid down sheets of tarpaulin all over the pitch, stitched them together with tape, and pinned them down. He stuck the heaters underneath, and in the moment of truth switched the whole contraption on. The tarpaulins started to rise with the hot air blowing through, but stayed held down tight. Karl was made up with himself, 'It's great is this!' he exclaimed. They all went away for the night and that's how they left it. And that's how they left it the next day too – nobody was coming in on Christmas Day. So, when it came to matchday, everybody turned up and realised the cold snap had frozen the generators on the heaters. The tarpaulin sheets had all frozen solid to the pitch. Game off.

Throughout the winter, training was frequently cancelled due to the pitches at Squires Gate being unplayable. But Holloway refused to allow excuses. The ball kept rolling one way or another. One week they trained on Blackpool beach. Ollie dragged his feet through the sand to form a crooked outline of a pitch and they had a kickabout, careful not to step on dog muck or rocks dragged up from the sea. He shouted instructions to one of his wingers, 'Stay out wide and hug the touchline!' A while later, as the training match progressed, the tide started to roll in and suddenly the touchline was underwater, the waves lapping over the player's boots. Everyone was beside themselves laughing. It might have been amateurish, but they used it in their favour.

The morale in the group stayed strong. The tales of Stanley Matthews running up and down Blackpool beach were legendary – and as Holloway always said, if it was good enough for Sir Stan, it was good enough for them. That was the attitude the team demanded of each other all the time. If a referee made a mistake and a player moaned, Steve Thompson would quip, 'Oh, look who must have had a bad game here then, trying to blame the ref?' On another day the snow shut Blackpool out of their training facility, so Ollie took them to the local casino and armed them with £20 each and they had a poker tournament well into the night. Spirits were incredibly high. Nobody in the dressing room had ever been part of such a tight-knit unit.

After a match at the Stadium of Light, the players were in a raucous mood on the team coach back home. They'd just beaten Sunderland 2-0, marking their third win in four.

They had 25 points from their opening 17 games and were eighth in the league. Due to the cancelled fixtures over Christmas, they had three games in hand over the two teams ahead of them, and at least one over the rest. It was the high point of the season. They were closer to the European spots than the relegation zone, but all the players could think of was getting to 40 points. At this rate they would reach the hallowed mark of near-certain safety after 28 games. But nobody thought it would be that easy.

Within the team, there was an awareness that they needed to be clear before the last game of the season, a trip to Old Trafford. With Sir Alex Ferguson at the helm, Manchester United were still the fiercest team in the country. Needing a result there would put Blackpool in a near-impossible position; they simply had to be safe by then. They were well ahead of their plan. They also had a sort of 'get out of jail free' card, as the scheduling quirk at the start of the season meant that in April, Blackpool had four home games in a row, and five in six. If they fell into trouble, they always had that to fall back on. That period became more and more important as losses began to pile up in the new year.

Goalkeeper Matt Gilks suffered a long-term injury and his replacement, Richard Kingson, struggled badly in his place. Rumours still abound that they had the chance to sign Shay Given on loan, who was by then in his late prime but had played 35 games in the league for Manchester City the year before. Nobody seems to know the full truth of the deal. It was reported City had said no because Given was registered in their Europa League squad, whereas a source inside Blackpool said that both Karl Oyston and Ian Holloway agreed the wages were too high a cost to pay.

Players recall hearing he had done a medical, but however far negotiations got it was never that close to being completed. It was no secret that the defence was their biggest weakness and relying instead on Kingson only exacerbated the issue. Without another fit goalkeeper, they tasked 20-year-old Mark Halstead and 18-year-old Chris Kettings to back up on the bench. Neither had played a single minute of professional football. Halstead was thrust into action in a 3-1 loss to Chelsea after Kingson came off injured, although he was back for the next game.

Their only win from the turn of the year to late February was another famous night at Bloomfield Road. They beat Liverpool again, in Kenny Dalglish's first game back in charge, to pull off the double over the Reds. They were seeking another big-name scalp a fortnight later, this time in the rearranged fixture against Manchester United at home. They were up for the game. They came out with the old style and swagger they had missed and took a 2-0 lead into the interval. They should have had a third, with one of the most outrageous penalty decisions not given their way when Rafael clattered attacker Luke Varney, clean through in the box. United brought on their wealth of attacking talent from the bench. Ryan Giggs and super-sub Javier Hernández entered the game. They sent wave after wave of attack and got a goal back with 18 minutes to go. Ferguson's United team were inevitable. It took just another two minutes for the equaliser. Blackpool held on as best they could, but there was no stopping the force in front of them, and Dimitar Berbatov twisted the knife in with the winning goal in the 88th minute. It was a devastating blow. They were treated to cold showers after the game as the boiler had broken. Blackpool were in freefall.

The January transfer window had looked like a mere luxury at one stage. Now, it felt like a vital necessity to boost the team and keep their heads above water. Fans were eager for the club to spend more. Safety was still well within their grasp, which would bestow upon them another huge cash windfall. Spending money on just one or two more first-team players was surely a risk well worth taking to get over the line. Typically, Karl Oyston turned to the loan market instead. They borrowed Jason Puncheon from League One Southampton, although he turned out to be one of their best signings of the season. They also signed Salaheddine Sbaï from French club Nimes, who was described as so far off the pace in training that the other players actually got angry with him, and at Holloway for bringing him in. The fans never caught sight of him; he never so much as made the bench, never mind getting on the pitch.

When it came to deadline day, the chaos and randomness from the first transfer window reappeared at Bloomfield Road. They hadn't learned from their mistakes. They were always playing catch-up and were now in the dreaded January window, which was 'for suckers', according to Karl. Anyone who was available probably wouldn't be any good, or else why would their club let them leave halfway through the season? It wasn't as if Blackpool were beating down doors with offers too good to refuse. When signings did arrive, they had no time to settle. Better-equipped clubs had translators for foreign players. They had liaison officers whose job it was to find flats and houses, schools for the kids, and everything right down to local nail salons for their wives or girlfriends. It was all taken care of, or just a phone call away. At Blackpool it was a quick hello, badly translated if you were foreign, and a short tour around the dilapidated training ground. The language barrier for one foreign signing caused immediate problems when he asked for a recommendation for a massage. He was told where he could get a proper sports massage, or where he could get a massage of the *other* sort. The latter was what he was after, but in a mix-up the former was where he was sent. The club got an angry phone call asking them to please explain to the player to put some clothes on.

The perils of transfer deadline day and how difficult it is for clubs like Blackpool can be seen nowhere better than their signing of Sergei Kornilenko. He wasn't on the club's radar, but on deadline day he was in London and his agent was pushing to get a move for him, so he called Blackpool. 'I've got a centre-forward here and he's in London.' That was the main selling point. Does he have two legs and is he in the country to get everything signed in time? Holloway watched a video of his highlights and gave the approval. Nobody at the club could speak his language. Nor did anybody at the club know that he wasn't in shape and that he was a smoker who liked a night out. His Blackpool career finished in the summer, playing six games without so much as a sniff at goal.

Other more familiar names, James Beattie and Andy Reid, didn't fare much better. Both worked hard in training and got on with the rest of the players, but weren't fit enough and were long past their best. Their best bit of business was fending off bids for Charlie Adam, but Blackpool's refusal to sell him to Liverpool also created some friction within the dressing room. They were supposed to be a selling team. The only way they had been able to convince Adam to sign was with the promise they would accept a bid if a bigger team came in for him. It was the pitch they gave to almost all their best signings. Most were cast-offs from bigger teams, used to higher wages. Sign for Blackpool and in return you'll get more playing time and play attacking football. If you impress, then you can earn more money when a club in a higher division comes calling. Internally, it felt like a broken promise not to sell him. But at the same time, everyone knew they wouldn't be able to replace him halfway through the season, even if they weren't averse to spending money. After the window closed, fans let out a sigh of relief.

Results continued to go against Blackpool, and Holloway took a trip abroad to search for new ideas. In the late March international break, he went to Spain to watch the national team train, who were on top of the world following dominant European Championship and World Cup wins. He also visited Real Madrid, Atlético Madrid and Getafe. On his return to Blackpool, he told his players, 'This switching thing, hitting the long switch, the rest of the league are on to us now, we need to keep the ball.' They were losing games and Holloway had to look for solutions, but his players questioned such a large change with eight games left in the season. They were moving away from their base attacking tactic, what everything else revolved around. In the first match back from the break, they lost 3-0 to Fulham. Fans came away enraged by a misplaced pass from James Beattie going backwards from the halfway line, which played in the opposition attacker to score. It would be oversimplifying things to suggest a sudden penchant for overpassing made them lose, but whatever they were trying to do, it didn't work.

Their third to last game of the season was away at Tottenham. By now they were desperate for wins to give them distance from the relegation zone, which they were only clear of by one goal on goal difference. Their last taste of victory had been the home fixture against Spurs in February, where they'd pulled off a magnificent 3-1 upset. It had been a night to remember for more than one reason, as Brett Ormerod broke his duck for the season. With his goal, he became the first player to score for Blackpool in all four divisions. He had fallen out of favour earlier in the year and the chance at history looked like it might pass him by. Everywhere he went, people brought it up in conversation, it became a cloud hanging over him. But in one of their finest victories of the season, he'd finally done it. He had scored so many memorable goals over the years, not least the winner at Wembley to get Blackpool to the Premier League. It was only fitting he get one more.

The return at White Hart Lane came at a point in the season where fans could no longer settle and enjoy the game. Performances were no longer relevant, just the score. Every point was crucial. In the 76th minute Blackpool won a penalty, offering a chance to break the deadlock. Charlie Adam took the ball, looking to score against the team he'd nearly joined. Tottenham had called half an hour before the window closed, audaciously hoping to push through a deal. Adam and his agent were pushing Oyston to accept, but he put the phone down on Spurs chairman Daniel Levy, refusing to entertain the sub-standard offer at such a late stage. Adam put the ball on the penalty spot, and missed. The resulting corner from the goalkeeper's save produced a goalmouth scramble, and improbably, Tottenham conceded their second penalty in less than a minute. Striker DJ Campbell went to pick up the ball. Adam grabbed it off him. There was no debate. He was the captain; he was the penalty taker. He placed the ball on the spot once again, then placed it in the exact opposite corner. As he ran to the Blackpool fans and smashed the badge on his shirt, it looked as if tears were in his eyes. Whether they could stay in the Premier League or were doomed to relegation, this was his last dance in a tangerine shirt. There was no doubt a move would eventually be arranged in the summer.

The win would have given Blackpool some breathing room, but they were undone by an 89th-minute equaliser by Jermain Defoe, who had built a career out of dashing hopes in similar fashion. Blackpool had one last home game, and they beat Bolton in a thrilling, back and forth encounter which ended 4-3. Adam scored the winner. It gave them a chance of survival on the day, but other results went against them. It was going to come down to Old Trafford. It was going to come down to getting a result against the champions, who were unbeaten at home all season. They'd played 28 home games in all competitions, winning 25 and drawing 3. Blackpool needed one more miracle.

The week ahead of the game was disastrous. The club had to make decisions on contracts, even with one fixture still to play, due to unfortunate wording in the small print. They were Championship contracts, signed in previous seasons. They had to decide whether or not to pick up the one-year option that many players had on their deals by the third Thursday of May – after the lower leagues stopped playing, but with one more fixture still left in the Premier League. Instead of rousing, motivational speeches, players were hearing whether or not they would even be at the club the next season. The players in question were mostly senior ones, so the decision to extend their contracts was easy. Although, after a season in which they had defied all odds to still have a chance of survival, it was an unhelpful reminder that they were about to be significantly underpaid for another year. Ormerod, included in the team at Old Trafford, was told his option was not being taken up. They would discuss a new deal but on much less favourable terms.

There were more distractions, with much talk surrounding Manchester United's team selection. They had already won the Premier League but still had the Champions League Final to play. Blackpool fans hoped heavy resting would be on the agenda, but United were warned they would face fines if they rotated their squad too heavily. Holloway hinted that Fergie would want to put a strong team out anyway to help his friend and compatriot Alex McLeish, who was in charge of relegation rivals Birmingham. Holloway put on a brave face to the media, 'In all of this wonderful euphoria we had from playing so well last weekend and giving ourselves a chance in the last game, I've had to then tell certain people that you haven't got a contract next year. Or I'm taking up your option, and that option might not be as good as they want, so it's slightly demotivating. So, we'll see if I'm any good or not as a motivator, because we've got to go to the champions and put up a fantastic fist and try and do what nobody has done so far and win. And if we do, they might get fined! Because we're rubbish and we shouldn't beat them. So, there we go, that's the week I'm having. It's belting, isn't it?'

When he was at Leicester, Holloway had gone into the final game of the season fighting to avoid the drop to League One. Once the final whistle blew, they were relegated by a single point. They had drawn with Stoke 0-0. Scoring one goal would have kept them up. That wasn't going to happen again. His rejuvenation at Blackpool had earned them plaudits as the nation's second team. Fans were almost tired of hearing how they were a 'breath of fresh air'.

The first time Holloway had ever brought an extra defender on to protect a result was in a game at Everton, after they had come from behind to take the lead 3-2 in a thrilling spectacle. Holloway replaced two attackers with a centre-back and defensive midfielder. Everton proceeded to score three goals in the next ten minutes. He only tried it once more, at Tottenham immediately after Charlie scored his penalty. It still couldn't stop the late equaliser. Instead, the usual tactic defending a lead was to keep attacking in the hope they could score more on the break and build a safer cushion. Blackpool's ethos was the reason they had won so many games and become the talk of the world in doing so. They looked back on some of the last-minute goals they conceded, particularly at Lancashire rivals Blackburn and Bolton, as agonising points dropped. With better fitness levels and more competitive squad depth, those could have been avoided, regardless of tactical tweaks. But the Premier League had fallen in love with everything tangerine. They were fearless. Their freedom loosened players to be their best selves on the pitch. It shocked new arrivals. In one early game Andy Reid was subbed off and laughed to himself as he went to the bench, 'I've just played a fucking one-two with my own centre-back at the edge of their box!' That was the Blackpool way, and they weren't going to do anything differently just because they were playing the champions.

Predictably, Manchester United took the lead, midway through the first half. The mountain in front of Blackpool grew taller, but Charlie Adam wasn't finished, and he recreated his Wembley masterclass with a free kick that curled around the United wall and nestled into the bottom corner. The sides entered half-time level. In the second half, a brilliant attacking move saw Gary Taylor-Fletcher skilfully flick the ball from the back of his foot into the goal. The final act was setting up to tell a heroic story. But there was an agonising amount of football still to play. As fans celebrated the lead in the away end, fuelled by a mixture of joy, exhilaration and booze, one staff member on the bench noticed something. For the first time in the game, Alex Ferguson got out of his seat and went all the way to the end of his technical box to deliver a message to his players. Some had been asking the 'Pool players at half-time what the other results were, professing their hope that they could stay up. After that word from the manager, they rediscovered their killer instinct.

Blackpool dropped deeper and deeper, an inevitability that couldn't be reversed no matter how much Holloway pleaded with his team to push forward. Ferguson subbed on ex-England striker Michael Owen. United piled the pressure on and got the equaliser, then they took the lead, and then they scored a fourth. Blackpool were pummelled. Holloway looked at his bench. Ferguson brought current England striker Wayne Rooney on as a substitute. Ian Holloway could only counter with Luke Varney and Brett Ormerod. The whistle blew and Blackpool were doomed to their fate. As they walked off the pitch, the Old Trafford crowd of 75,000 gave them a standing ovation.

In the ten years since Blackpool's relegation, no team has gone down with as many points. The year before Blackpool joined, just 31 was enough. They got 39; 39 points and ten wins. They threw aside mockery from pundits before the season that they would fail to reach Derby's infamous record-low total of 11. What made it all the more cruel was the letter Ian Holloway received from the Premier League after the season finished. It showed an alternative league table, without obvious refereeing mistakes, that had Blackpool nine points better off and comfortably safe.

Blackpool had crashed the party. For the first time in decades, everyone knew who they were and what they were about. They had developed a style that was the envy of fans around the country. And they came so close. 'We'll be back!' fans shouted defiantly as they left the stadium. They sang one last rendition of 'This is the best trip I've ever been on', which had become the backing song to their journey under Holloway. They didn't know then that the best trip had finished. Nobody could see what was about to come.

Chapter 3

The Fall

AFTER RELEGATION, Ian Holloway was able to rebuild his squad despite the departures of arguably his three best players. Charlie Adam finally got his dream move to Liverpool, and DJ Campbell and David Vaughan also departed. Unexpectedly, the club reached new deals with Stephen Crainey and Matt Gilks, who at one time were thought to have Premier League interest. They, along with a handful of others, were spared the indignity of the usual 50 per cent pay cut on relegation, with help from Holloway fighting their corner.

There was plenty of optimism that Blackpool could make an immediate return. They were one of the most cash-rich teams in the entire league. The Championship was littered with big clubs with high expectations, and now Blackpool could puff their chest out and claim to be one of them. As usual though, it was an underwhelming start to the summer. The first signing was Bojan Djordjic, a name most familiar with fans of the *Championship Manager* video game series. His inflated ability in the 2001/02 edition had made him a cult favourite, but in real life his career had gone downhill since leaving Manchester United in 2005.

He'd been struggling for games in Hungary before joining Blackpool on a free transfer. It wasn't the sort of proven name fans were hoping to see, but key signings later arrived by way of Kevin Phillips and Barry Ferguson, two vastly experienced and respected veterans. They slotted right into the team, and they weren't cheap either. Earning between £15,000 and £18,000 a week each, they were on far more than any player had been getting in the Premier League.

These were the signings Karl Oyston pointed to over and over again in defence of Blackpool's spending record, but overall, the wage bill contracted sharply. Despite making the second-highest profit in the Championship that year at £15.5m pre-tax, they had only the 16th-highest budget. Their wages to turnover ratio was by far the lowest in the league, at 42 per cent. But they had young, talented players. They snagged Tom Ince from Liverpool after Holloway nearly beat Paul Ince's door down trying to convince him he could take his son to the next level. They were able to attract quality players on loan, fending off competition to get Callum McManaman and Jonjo Shelvey. They added Lomana LuaLua on a free transfer. It barely made a dent in the profit from parachute payments and player sales, but they rebuilt a very competitive side on the fly.

A new midfield was crafted with the short passing and interplay skills of Ferguson, fellow new signing Ángel Martínez, and Ludovic Sylvestre, who had joined in the Premier League and was ready to break through as a regular starter. Throughout the pitch, Blackpool had players who wanted the ball. Players who could keep it and move it when they got it. Holloway wanted to slow the tempo down, just slightly, and now he had a full summer to make his tweaks. It was a move motivated by a need to improve defensively. The way he saw it, if you were in possession, you couldn't concede. The players took to their new, evolved identity. They had lost their best men and suffered a painful relegation, but they were ready to push on.

The first half of the season was mostly inconsistent. Then, at the turn of the new year, Blackpool roared forward by winning 11 of their last 22 games, only losing four. Another promotion looked on the cards. Then in March, the story broke that changed everything for the club. Some fans had been eagerly anticipating the day the 2011 accounts were to be filed online, revealing all the details of the money coming in and out during the Premier League season. Everyone could digest just how much cash Blackpool were sitting on. The club stuck up a press release on the official website beforehand, patting themselves on the back. It boasted of the massive £50m in turnover they had achieved. What it didn't mention, which the accounts laid out in black ink for everyone to see, was that Owen Oyston had paid himself £11m.

It was headline news. Blackpool fans were disgusted and outraged, and the football world was right behind them. It featured in a full two-page spread in the *Daily Mail*. The team's wage bill for the Premier League season was a little over £12m, meaning Oyston had earned almost as much as the entire team combined in basic salary. He wasn't just the highest-paid person at Blackpool, he earned more than any player in British football. The fall-out was immense. Online message boards lit up in chaos with fans spewing their venom and anger at the betrayal. 'At least Dick Turpin wore a mask,' wrote one supporter. The Oystons were nowhere to be found. Owen rarely spoke to the media and Karl had fled the country on a conveniently well-timed holiday. A week later, the team travelled down to Peterborough for an away game, on a push for promotion in the latter stages of the season. When they arrived, the club's two credit cards were both declined. Holloway had to offer to foot the bill to get the players into their rooms, although they were able to arrange a later payment instead. The club vehemently denied the situation to the press, blaming a technical issue at the hotel. Karl was still abroad when the incident occurred, leading to claims he'd maxed out the card. Club secretary Matt Williams gave this version of events; however, Karl Oyston denied this. According to Karl, the card was held by his PA and was used on coach hire, hotel booking, and any other day-to-day operations at the football club. This was supported by club financial controller Rod Dyer. All the cards got maxed out often due to relatively small limits. Whatever the truth, it was certainly a humiliating turn of events coming days after Owen's bonus hit the news.

When Karl eventually did give an interview on the situation, he did little to ease the groundswell of criticism. Fighting back, he tried to explain that the money had not gone directly to his father, rather to a company called Zabaxe (which was wholly owned by his father). He claimed it had been done for sound tax planning reasons. This seems to have been a half-truth. Putting it into Zabaxe, instead of a direct payment to Owen, resulted in a lower corporation tax bill rather than PAYE as salary – but that helped Owen, not the club. It was later revealed that Zabaxe paid £2,589,854 in corporation tax, a negligible difference to the sum Blackpool would have owed if they kept the money. Karl then tried to pass it off as a 'repayment'. A return on all the money Owen had put in over the years. If it was a repayment, it was of an amount totted up in his head. There was no loan, no agreement, no number given in the accounts to back it up. Owen later produced seven invoices from Zabaxe over the 'many years' of work they had done, mostly for small sums. Overall, it amounted to £450,000, quite a bit short of the £11m he took. He tried to claim it was backdated payment for his years acting as a consultant, but this didn't square with the true nature of the power structure within. Karl now openly speaks about how he constantly had to keep Owen away from business matters, making apologies for him when he did manage to intrude. They both insisted that the money hadn't disappeared. They would happily lend the club the money if it needed it, interest-free, for a 'rainy day'. Behind the scenes, however, the true nature of the payment was never ambiguous. Owen Oyston wanted it for himself.

Owen wrote to his financial advisors beforehand, and said, 'As you are aware, I have served 25 years in the harness of Blackpool FC and in the initial year saved them from extinction, loaned money interest-free, converted loans into shares to strengthen its balance sheet, made temporary loans every time they were in trouble, again interest-free, and provided financial support for their borrowings. So now after the success of the Premier League and the strong financial position of the Club, the chairman is putting down on the agenda a proposal that certain bonuses are paid.'

The next day, Owen emailed Karl with a proposal that he would receive £5m. A month later, when Karl notified the Latvian side of the board about the impending transfer, the figure had ballooned to £11m. Normunds Malnacs, Valeri Belokon's right-hand man, was incredulous, replying, 'First, how could you decide on making £11m worth of emolument to one shareholder, without the other major shareholder's approval or at least a meaningful discussion?! This is out of any acceptable corporate governance norms, even without mentioning the moral aspect of the transaction!'

The payment went through despite their protests, and weeks later when it was made public, Blackpool fans were asking themselves the same questions. Karl was doing his best to deflect criticism, but in the end, he couldn't help himself. He finished an interview with *The Guardian* by sniping, 'But frankly, after the way he has supported the club all these years, if it was an £11m salary to my father, so what?'

The Oystons moved money around freely from company to company. It was legal, but fans were still furious that they were taking it out of the football club, when they should have been reinvesting and building a legacy with the Premier League war chest. Speaking now, Sam Oyston – who at 18 was given a job managing the new club hotel built into the stadium – admitted the whole family used the football club as a personal bank account. They all took relatively small salaries, but abused the expenses system to put all sorts of luxuries on to the club card. In an effort to reduce their personal tax bill, everything was charged as expenses. All the way from vehicles to the endless restaurant and bar tabs that were listed as 'business meetings'. Owen expensed whatever he could, including his accommodation at the hotel and personal staff, right down to gardeners at his house.

Owen used the football club and hotel income to fund his lavish lifestyle. It helped purchase a new estate at Quernmore Park Hall that he wanted. It funded shopping trips for the latest girl on his arm. He fed off the ego trip he got by throwing cash around. He left large tips around town to show how rich and powerful he was. On more than one occasion at the club hotel, a guest came to reception to ask why an old man had given them a £50 note, thinking they were a concierge, because they politely held a door open for him. Karl estimated Owen had 40 or 50 different 'PAs' who all left the club a lot happier than they came in. One in particular used Owen spectacularly. She had cosied up to him enough that he bought her an Audi TT. She left but came back some time later after the money dried up. She had sold the car and managed to squeeze another one out of him, this time a new BMW. He also bought her a house. A few months later she left again and married somebody else. She was set up for life.

Immediately after the money went into Zabaxe, it started flowing out. The Oyston business empire was crumbling, and loss-making businesses needed propping up. It was sent to various other ventures, some already established, others new vanity projects. Two years later, Zabaxe had £4.7m of the £11m remaining in the bank. It funded Owen's various attempts to enter the fashion world. He'd been setting up a whole host of fashion companies for years, all on the whims of his latest business meeting, where he would try to wine and dine anyone in earshot. On 23 September 2011, several such companies were incorporated with an 18-year-old girl listed as the only director. Her father owned a security firm that handled matchday operations and worked with Owen Oyston for years. She was trying to make it as a fashion designer, and has gone on to work in the industry, which is why Owen used her as the front. Speaking now, another director on the board claimed Owen was less interested in the opportunity to develop such companies, and more interested in using them to surround himself with models, luring them into his web with photo shoots held at his house.

'I own a fashion company,' was described as Owen's chat-up line. He promised trips to China to look for factories, and elaborate shoots in Turkey and South Africa. He used it as an expensable excuse to travel around the world. Using the money from Blackpool FC, Zabaxe loaned one such company, House of Roma, over half a million pounds. It never traded. It was all spent on 'administrative expenses'. Not one single penny was returned. Owen worked with designer Nadine Merabi, before she found a better business partner. It was another effort to show he was working with creative, talented people, 'so it doesn't look like he's a creepy old man', the same director added.

By 2017, £5,584,749 was loaned to 11 different Oyston-owned companies. The money has never been repaid. From Zabaxe, with what little remained of the BFC money in its bank, Owen Oyston also took a personal loan of £186,700. Karl Oyston took a loan of £147,272. Sam Oyston took a loan of £59,818. Sam alleges that all three loans were actually Owen's, taking money out in the name of others. On top of that was around £700,000 left unaccounted for, listed ambiguously as 'other debtors'. The £11m payment dwindled and dwindled every year until 2017, when the company had £70,000 left in the bank. There was nothing left.

The Zabaxe payment was just the tip of the iceberg. Year after year, more and more money was transferred out of Blackpool FC and into Segesta, Owen's holding company which owned the club and associated assets. By 2018, the money taken out had reached £30.1m, dubiously labelled as a 'loan'. The Oystons told inquisitive fans and journalists this money was being spent on player wages and stadium development. But that did little to quell outside suspicion that the money wasn't being used quite as advertised, and the lack of transparency in the accounts made it impossible for outside observers to verify.

The Premier League money went into Blackpool FC and was transferred to Segesta shortly after, before many millions were loaned out to Owen's other companies. The companies could lay no claim to offering football-related services. Over the years, £5.5m was rerouted to these other businesses, mostly in unsecured, interest-free loans, with little prospect of return. One such recipient was *Yorkshire Ridings* magazine, which promptly went out of business. In 2013, Segesta loaned Natfarm – another Owen Oyston-controlled company – £1.8m. Owen had already loaned the company £1.2m himself, and as the Segesta money went in, his loan reduced to £1. There was little other way of reading the accounts than to presume Owen had used Blackpool FC's money to pay off his own debt to a separate, loss-making company he owned. With each year, some loans were paid off, but new ones began – never to be returned.

All of this was to play out in the future. By the end of the 2011/12 season, amidst the furore in the press and from the fans regarding Owen's £11m payment, Blackpool were quietly surging in the league. They secured a spot in the play-offs yet again, overcoming Birmingham 3-2 on aggregate in the semi-final to book a return to Wembley. The challenge was the toughest yet – Sam Allardyce's West Ham United, who had thrown money at the Championship in hopes of an immediate return to the Premier League. They had finished in third place, 11 points higher than Blackpool. Holloway's men played some scintillating football on the day, especially in the second half as their nerves settled down. For a prolonged spell they knocked the ball around with ease, and West Ham were chasing shadows.

It was one of the best displays of football they had produced, but it wasn't enough. They squandered chance after chance, and then Ricardo Vaz Tê scored on the break in the 87th minute to win the game 2-1 for West Ham.

Holloway privately told a reporter in the Wembley tunnels after the loss that he was going to resign. It had been the most exhilarating journey of his career, but an equally as exhausting one. He could see the clock ticking towards an ugly end. Senior players were getting older. He still believed they had plenty to offer, but Karl told him that once their contracts expired in a year's time, he was going to offer them new contracts halving their current wages. There was one year left before the parachute payments declined from £16m to £8m. Despite the club still raking in huge profits, he wanted the playing budget to see a similar drop.

It didn't take much foresight to recognise the whole thing was about to fall apart. In the moment, part of Holloway recognised the time was right for him to leave. It had been such a heartbreaking and undeserved loss at Wembley, but he'd still be going out a hero and on something of a high. As the squad departed for the off-season break, he was able to take stock and reflect on his decision. Ultimately, he opted to stay for the 2012/13 season. It didn't take long for him to realise he'd made a mistake. The money dried up. Isaiah Osbourne was signed for £250,000 to replace the departing Keith Southern, but other than that it was a long list of free transfers who barely played a minute. The likes of Brice Irie-Bi, Adda Djeziri, James Caton and Jake Caprice are names that even diehard Blackpool fans will struggle to remember. Holloway always had a volatile approach to the transfer market, unearthing a few diamonds but bringing in many more flops. That summer, the diamonds failed to materialise. The club was still without a real recruitment system. The year before, he had signed a forward from America called Craig Sutherland on the recommendation of his wife, Kim. An agent had sent over a DVD of his highlights and she had watched it one night, impressed. He didn't score a single goal for Blackpool before being released (but not before tweeting a picture of his £1,000 weekly wages, which had been delivered to him in two sandwich bags entirely in pound coins). That approach to the transfer market, coupled with Karl Oyston's fingers clenching tighter and tighter on the club wallet, did not equate to success.

Holloway often talked about wanting to develop young players, trying to push for the club to be a conveyor belt for talent. He scrapped the reserve team and replaced it with a 'development squad', which ended up bloated with 18 to 23-year-olds who weren't playing enough football. It was another half-measured approach. The club didn't have the infrastructure to operate the way he wanted. Everything came from him and Steve Thompson. They ran themselves into the ground getting things prepared for the first team and couldn't handle a second squad of young players too. The players deserved proper attention and monitoring, regular games either in a reserve league or out on loan. Holloway had something of a blueprint to build a long-term structure, but he needed help. Instead, he was left isolated.

The 2012/13 season started spectacularly, and it looked as if Holloway had reinvented his squad once more. Three wins from three, culminating in a 6-0 win over Ipswich, shot them to the top of the table. Behind the scenes, however, things were falling apart. The constant battles with Karl had finally worn Holloway down. 'I used to argue over people or money, people or money, all the time. I would fight for people. He would fight for money,' he later said. Holloway alleged that Karl had been trying to force him out, unhappy with the contract he was on. According to sources from the club, he was the highest earner and hadn't received as large a pay cut upon relegation as many players had. While Karl was cutting costs on the playing side, he still had a manager on what he saw as Premier League wages. Not only did he not want to pay him, he knew if any other club poached him they would have to write a cheque for what was left on his deal. 'We gotta get you to Arsenal,' Holloway said Karl constantly told him. He alleged Karl's plan was to push him out by informing him of his grand plan to slash wages, 'He wanted to sell me to get me out of that contract. That's what he did in the end. I got all sorts of stick for leaving, but I was not gonna stay there and see all those players be offered a lot less than what they were on before I started, and I'm being touted around, being sold here and there. Was that the right time to leave? No, not really. I wanted to build something for the club, for the people, for myself. To keep going and going and have a brand of football to play. Unfortunately, that was never going to happen in the end.'

Karl followed through on his warning the next summer. The senior members of the squad, who had been with the team since Holloway joined, were offered pay cuts at the end of the season. Most were informed of their offer by text. When they took time to mull the decision over and speak with other teams, they were given a second offer, even worse than the first. For Gary Taylor-Fletcher, his offer of a 50 per cent pay cut turned into a proposed 65 per cent reduction. 'Nobody's going to want you,' Karl would say in negotiations. The senior players were all around 30 years of age and entering their late primes, but most proved him wrong in their next stops. Taylor-Fletcher won promotion with Leicester, and Stephen Crainey played in the FA Cup semi-final at Wembley for Wigan. During negotiations they would walk into his office and see he was on a fans' message board, where he posted regularly under pseudonyms and got into long, petty arguments with supporters. If he was on the website, they knew he would be in a bad mood and the talks would go poorly. Holloway didn't want to stick around to see his players dragged through that process.

One of the final straws was failing to bring back a familiar favourite, as Holloway was desperate to sign DJ Campbell again. In three spells at Bloomfield Road, he'd scored at a rate of nearly one goal every two games. He was proven not only in the Championship, but in the Premier League too. He'd always played his best football under Holloway and was as close to a sure thing as you could get. It would cost another million, but Karl wouldn't budge. Instead, he went to Ipswich on loan and scored 10 goals in 17 games. Holloway couldn't fight any more battles. He made the decision he was going to leave.

There are, of course, two sides to this story. Holloway alleged that Karl was touting him around, but he was doing a good-enough job of that himself. Sometime at the start of the 2012/13 season he asked his agent to find him a new job. He talked with Ipswich and Blackburn, at least in an informal capacity. Wolves were interested, but he was put off by what he perceived to be unfair treatment of ex-manager Mick McCarthy. One person with knowledge of the situation also said he interviewed for the Burnley job before they gave it to Sean Dyche. While there had been expectations in the summer from fans that Holloway may depart for greener pastures, there would have been a sense of betrayal at watching him jump ship for their Lancashire rivals. The chairman at the time, Barry Kilby, confirmed the interview took place, but Holloway – while happy to confirm he had spoken to the other clubs – refuted the story that he'd talked with Burnley. Whatever the case, the writing was on the wall. He was leaving, it was just a matter of where he would end up.

After their excellent start, the problems behind the scenes became apparent on the pitch and Blackpool won just two of their next ten games. They skidded down the league table. The team looked disjointed, and Holloway bereft of ideas. He played down stories in the media that he was eyeing other jobs and played up boos from a handful of supporters. One particular confrontation with a fan who had heckled him from his seat, as the team laboured on the pitch, seemed to affect him more than it should have. His departure finally came the night before a game against Derby. He was taking training at Squires Gate when local journalists got a tip that he was saying his goodbyes to the players, giving an emotional speech about his reasons for leaving. They rushed to the training ground. After some time waiting outside, they saw Kim drive out of the complex in an otherwise empty car. They waited some more, hoping to catch Holloway himself. Later, a player drove past and stopped. 'Is Holloway still in there?' one of the journalists asked. 'No, he's gone, he's just gone in Kim's car,' they replied. Somebody later reported that they had seen Kim pull over further down the road, where Holloway then emerged from his hiding place in the boot. The story became legendary in the years since, with some promising it was true and others claiming embellishment. Holloway himself finally confirmed that it was only a slight exaggeration. He'd actually crouched down in the front of the car to hide. It's an amusing story to look back on now, but after the journey that had come before it, it was an undignified end.

Whispers began to spread online, but the fans didn't find out for sure until the following morning, the day of the Derby game. They felt blindsided. Steve Thompson felt ready to take charge, and all the preparations had been put in place beforehand, but they got hammered 4-1. There was initial anger over the manner of the exit, although most seemed to appreciate that even if it wasn't the cleanest break, Holloway had left for a much better opportunity at Crystal Palace, where he went on to win promotion to the Premier League once again. The players weren't surprised. They were also starting to plan for futures elsewhere. The team had always maintained a strong spirit in the dressing room, and nobody complained about the oddities of working for Blackpool FC. Most had been at bigger teams before and ultimately failed to maintain a regular place in the starting line up, but they had revitalised their career under Holloway. They got on with washing their own kit, eating microwave supermarket meals, and all the other quirks that came with playing for the club. Kevin Phillips, who at 38 years old followed a strict diet that kept him in better shape than anybody else at the club, commuted in from Birmingham. He needed to eat after the drive, but he was forced to go to a McDonald's drive-through just to get plain porridge. It wasn't what he was used to, but he made it work. That was the attitude of the whole squad.

Things started to change as the players realised the legacy they wanted to build was being frittered away. They followed the news, as the fans did. Discontent rumbled after the story broke of Owen Oyston's £11m payday. Why did they still have to wash their own kit and train at Squires Gate while the owner was getting richer and richer? Why did they have to accept sub-standard contracts with the promise of generous bonuses, if the owner took the biggest share of the rewards? They saw how tired Holloway had become and felt sorry for him. Towards the end, he admitted in conversations with them, 'I don't know how long I can keep battling him, it's wearing me out. I don't know whether I can change that man.' 'Nobody's going to change him,' one player replied. Nobody was prouder of what Blackpool had achieved than the manager and players in the dressing room. That time was now over. Jimmy Armfield, who wasn't officially a director on the board but was often present to lend advice, signed off the era in a typically gracious way. He gave Holloway a card on which he wrote, 'Thank you for the days in the sun.'

The club was at a crossroads. The day was always going to come when Holloway would leave, but because of the lack of structure behind the scenes there wasn't much of a succession plan. The new manager would have to hit the ground running without a support team ready to help him. Each managerial hire was crucial. They weren't just the head coach, but the head of recruitment too. Michael Appleton was chosen after an impressive stint at Portsmouth, during which he had endured through incredible financial difficulties at the club. Appleton leapt at the chance. He did little homework; the interview came quickly and took place at Karl Oyston's house. Appleton brought over his trusted number two, Ashley Westwood. Neither saw the training ground before signing the paperwork. They saw Blackpool as an opportunity to jump from a situation where they were handcuffed every day, at a club facing constant struggles to keep the lights on. Now they would be at a team not only a division higher, but only recently out of the Premier League. They were completely caught off guard when they turned up to work at Squires Gate. Appleton held an early press conference in the manager's office at the training ground. Autumn was turning to winter and the temperature in Blackpool was dropping. He cranked up the heating, but when he did so the fuse blew and the lights went out. The kit man informed him the power could only handle heat or light, but not both at the same time. 'Well, we're just gonna have to do it in the dark,' he told the journalists.

As Appleton walked through the portacabin complex, navigating around the buckets collecting rain leaking through the roof, he was met with a group of players who had fostered a deep connection with Ian Holloway. It made him insecure. If he saw a group of players together, he would ask them what they were doing, what they were talking about. He knew the shadow of Holloway loomed large and felt the pressure of being his successor. When Gary Taylor-Fletcher was ruled out for a game by the physio due to a hamstring strain, Appleton stormed into the treatment room. 'What's wrong with you, if it was Holloway you'd play wouldn't you!' he shouted. 'You've been tapped up, who's been calling to sign you?'

For their part, some of the players were upset that Steve Thompson hadn't been given the job. He'd always had a strong hand in training, running drills separately without Holloway's involvement. He was beloved. He had gone from coaching in the youth team, to promotion to the senior side, to assistant manager, and now finally felt ready for the main job. Not only did he not get it, he was effectively usurped in the hierarchy by Westwood, a fiery character who could at any time unleash a tirade on anyone in front of him.

Despite the loss of form, it was still early in the season and there was hope that if Appleton started quickly, Blackpool could launch another attack on the play-offs. Instead, they drew their first four games, playing a strikingly negative style of football in comparison to what they had been treating fans to under Holloway. The optimists pointed to the slow start Holloway had, also drawing his first four league games. Others were less convinced, not quite clear what Appleton was *trying* to do. Two wins and another draw followed. Blackpool were unbeaten in Appleton's first seven games, but results took a turn for the worse and they lost three of their next five going into Christmas. The January transfer window should have been an opportunity for the new manager to bring in his key players, to be backed by the chairman to stamp his identity on to the team. If it was ever going to work, he needed a chance to build what he wanted to build. But when he tried to talk players, he found Karl Oyston either unwilling to listen or impossible to even get hold of. A list of ten targets would see the first eight quickly crossed off and the bottom two marked as possibilities. When Ollie was hired, he managed to secure his top transfer targets in Charlie Adam, Neal Eardley and eventually DJ Campbell. Appleton wasn't so lucky. He had left Portsmouth in search of stability and ambition; he found neither at Blackpool.

The supporters were disillusioned with the results and performances on the pitch. When the story broke that Blackburn had interest in poaching Appleton, two months after he had taken the job, nobody was too upset. They were angry at the overall state of affairs, rather than out of any sense of loyalty to the manager. They didn't like the football being played, and the results were even worse.

Appleton wanted out. After a cup game away at Fulham at the start of January, sources within Blackpool said he left Craven Cottage and went straight to Euston station, instead of travelling back with the team. From there he made his way to the airport, got on a plane to India, and met with the owners of Blackburn. When Appleton and Westwood walked into Bloomfield Road again it was to inform Karl they were leaving. Karl wasn't offended by the nature of their departure and just laughed instead, telling them, 'You two are the best managerial team I've ever had because Blackburn are paying me to get rid of you, you've made me three grand every day you've been here!' Sixty-five days after joining, Appleton was out.

It was always going to be an extremely difficult task to find a manager capable of replacing Holloway, but his appointment had gone about as disastrously as it possibly could have. Reflecting back on his time at the club, Appleton said, 'I just made a poor judgement. I didn't do proper research on the Oystons, particularly Karl, who to this day is the most difficult man I've ever worked with. I could never get hold of him, and he wasn't willing to have sensible conversations. I found him to be very disrespectful, but I was in such a rush to get out of the environment I was in.'

The search for a new manager was on. Again. The shortlist was the same and the usual suspects all said no. Owen Coyle wanted to bring 'Team Owen' with him and bolster the backroom staff, which Karl wouldn't agree to. Sean O'Driscoll and Billy Davies both showed interest, but only to use the vacancy as leverage for applications elsewhere. O'Driscoll took the Bristol City job and Davies ended up back at Nottingham Forest. The man who really wanted the job was Paul Ince. He was already a mainstay at

Bloomfield Road as he watched his son Tom blossom into one of the most exciting talents outside the Premier League. Ince senior was the last man standing, so he was given the position in late February. A person close to Karl thought he got 'bored' during the process, unwilling to put in the work to meet with more candidates and thoroughly vet them. Ince was around, Karl's first few targets hadn't worked out, so he gave in.

Ince had a mixed reputation from his previous stints in management. However, staff at Blackpool were pleasantly surprised at his attitude when he took over. He rolled his sleeves up and got to work. Despite losing his first game, he was able to steady the ship and Blackpool only had two losses in their final 13. They finished the season comfortably clear of relegation, when at one point it looked like they were slipping close.

It had been a tumultuous year, one best confined to the history books, and a summer of great transition was to follow. Oyston handed out insulting offers and cut the playing budget as promised. Almost all the players from the promotion team departed for pastures new. Only goalkeeper Matt Gilks remained. Ince took what was left of his team out to Portugal for a pre-season camp. Karl and Matt Williams were in the area for the annual EFL chairman's conference, so the three met to discuss transfer targets. Ince suggested players such as Ross McCormack, a big-name Championship striker who a year later would sell for an eye-popping £11m. He was many orders of magnitude out of Blackpool's comfort zone. Karl nodded along to his suggestions, but immediately after the meeting turned to Williams and, out of Ince's earshot, said, 'Well we're not signing any of them.' The chairman and manager were at odds quickly. Ince promised an old player of his, Neal Bishop, that he would sign him and bring him into the team. Karl was infuriated with him, shouting 'You don't promise anything without my say so!' Bishop was a utility player that hardly broke the bank, but neither Oyston nor Ince had any trust in each other. The football club was Karl's, and he ran it his way and his way alone.

Despite not getting his transfer targets, Ince helmed the best-ever start to a new season in Blackpool's history, as they had a hugely successful beginning to the 2013/14 campaign. In their first six games they won five and drew one, including impressive wins over promotion-chasing teams such as Watford and recently relegated Reading. But most Blackpool fans watching thought the football they were playing was *awful*. Each win came with a great deal of luck. They were scraping through with 1-0 win after 1-0 win. Ince was confident in the results though, to the extent that some around the club started to think he'd gotten 'big-time'. His larger-than-life persona was starting to grate on others, and one department manager was shocked at how rudely he treated lower-level members of staff. He was known as the 'Guv'nor' during his playing days, which according to some was a nickname he'd given himself, and he still demanded the same adulation. At meals, staff had to wait to begin eating until he started. If anyone started eating their food before he did, he would fine them. They would crack jokes behind his back, 'Permission to eat, gaffer?' He was described as great company, but there were doubts he was the right man to lead a professional football club.

On a night out, at around 6am, it is alleged that Ince turned up drunk to a club in town called Flamingo. Well-known owner Basil Newby was at the front door with a bouncer, and apparently Ince walked past them and tried to get into the club. According to Newby, he attempted to stop him, trying to explain that all guests had to pay to come in. He says Ince shouted, 'I don't pay, don't you know who I fucking am?' Not a football fan in the slightest, Newby didn't. Ince was supposedly enraged, trying to push past the bouncer and get into the club, at one point ending up behind the closed-off reception. With the bouncer trying to calm him down and restrain him, Newby claims Ince took a swing, missing but punching Newby in the face instead. He was whisked off and an official from the football club confirmed that they arrived on the scene and managed to convince Newby to stay silent about the issue to the police and media.

The incident was kept out of the newspapers, but the supporters were still turning on the manager. The attacking football they'd enjoyed for years had become a distant memory. Ince further alienated himself in press conferences. He called 1-0 his 'favourite scoreline in football', and after a 1-1 draw commented, 'We ended up with a stretched game – they attacked, we attacked. I hate playing football like that, it's ridiculous.' Everything was defence first. Full-backs were berated for daring to go past the halfway line, everybody stuck to their positions. Tom Ince was the only player given any creative freedom and the only attacking strategy seemed to be hoping he would produce a moment of magic to score. It worked for a while, until it didn't. The luck ran out and the wheels fell off.

It started with an away victory at Bournemouth in the first game back after an international break. During a tight affair, Ince lost his temper completely in the dugout, erupting after a refereeing decision went against them. First, he threw a water bottle on to the floor, which bounced away and hit a fan in the stand. It was a complete accident, which didn't cause any injuries, and Ince immediately went over to her and apologised. The referee sent him off, and then things turned violent. Witnesses said Ince shouted at the fourth official, 'I'll fucking knock you out, you cunt!' and pushed him aggressively. He was hauled in front of an FA disciplinary hearing. His defence rested on calling the witnesses unreliable, because 'anybody that knows Paul Ince knows I don't ever use the "c" word'. The barrister questioned him, 'Is it fair to say, that maybe you didn't use that word, but a different word, and then proceeded to shove the official?' Ince replied, 'Yes, but I didn't call him the "c" word,' essentially admitting to the real breach of conduct. He was given the heavy penalty of a five-match stadium ban.

There was concern that Ince's lack of discipline would reflect in the dressing room and on to the pitch. The wins dried up and there came a flashpoint moment at Yeovil away, in their first game of December. Blackpool were 1-0 down, and then it was as if the entire team, manager, club, and all it entailed, lost its head all at once. Three players were sent off in injury time. Four days later they played Derby away and were demolished 5-1, with two more players getting red cards. Two brutal losses and five suspensions in four days. It was alarming.

The transfer window was coming up, but instead of the focus being on scouting potential recruits, Ince embarked on a tour around the country with his son. He had always acted as Tom's agent, and his talent had far outgrown Blackpool. Premier League clubs were interested, as were Inter Milan and Monaco. Blackpool fans watched on in bemusement as photos emerged of their manager sat in meetings with their best player, talking to other teams about selling him. When Charlie Adam had left, nobody thought Blackpool could replace him, but there was optimism that they could spend the money on fresh new faces to develop down the line. The optimism was well placed. Tom Ince came the other way from Liverpool and broke into the first team later that season. There *had* seemed to have been something of a conveyor belt of talent at Bloomfield Road. But those days were over. The supporters knew that once Tom left, more players would be sold. They had no confidence there would be a new young talent through the door. Once he went, that was it. It was a depressing thought. It marked the end of an era, although few could truly foresee just how dark the future was.

The Yeovil loss started an almost incomprehensibly bad run of form that extended well into future seasons. In the 12 months following that long journey down to the south coast, Blackpool played exactly 50 games and won just four. Four wins in an entire calendar year. They picked up 24 points from a possible 150. It was a scarily quick descent into relentless failure. They had gone from the darlings of football fans everywhere – earning promotion to the Premier League on the second-smallest budget in the Championship and taking on the best teams in the world, while playing entertaining, attacking football – to the sorriest football team in England.

Ince was sacked in January 2014. The fans turned on him as the losses piled up with no end in sight. His answers to the media left a great deal to be desired. Ince shifted blame and attempted to downplay the severity of the situation, with Blackpool now well and truly mired in a relegation fight. His last game ended in ugly scenes as he walked down the tunnel past jeering fans, spitting venom and bile.

To the shock of many, stalwart Steve Thompson was also shown the door. Many players and fans had wanted Thompson to get the main job. His nickname was Mr Blackpool because he had done so much for the club, seeking little recognition or reward. When he joined as youth team coach, the development system was barely functioning. It was completely ignored and neglected. The Oystons saw it only as a way to get a grant from the FA, who chipped in yearly for running costs. Blackpool's kids played games in mismatched shirts and shorts – whatever bit of kit they could get their hands on. Thompson would be first to arrive at Squires Gate in the morning and go through a regular routine to make the place presentable. The nets would fly through the night air and he had to retrieve them from the other end of the pitch. As he walked across the surface, he picked up cigarette butts and bottles of beer, the aftermath of people walking through or camping the night before. He got used to rolling his sleeves up and fixing things himself. He washed kits on his own time for no extra money. It became a family thing. His son Curtis was in the youth set-up and helped out the first-team squad in preparing their equipment. His daughter Stephanie took time out to make tea and sandwiches during training.

With the help of a few parents, Thompson repainted the interior of the facility. They got sponsors for the kits which paid for more maintenance work. Thompson drove down to Bloomfield Road and got his hands on as much memorabilia as he could carry. He wanted *his* walls to be lined with photos of legendary Blackpool players, so the youth players could have something to look up to. It was about putting some pride back into the place. He built it from the ground up. They were working with their hands tied behind their backs, with no support from the chairman's office. They weren't even allowed a running float and had to take money out of the vending machines to pay the referees on matchday. When he was promoted to the first team, the list of jobs he had to do only grew. He turned down an opportunity to join Holloway at Crystal Palace when he left. It hadn't been an easy fit working with Appleton and then Ince, but he laboured to make it work. After all he'd done for the club, he was sad, but not surprised, that it ended in a text message.

Managerless for the third time in a little over a year, Karl was struggling to find someone to take over. Nobody wanted the job. In the end, it was given in a caretaker capacity to Barry Ferguson, who despite declining playing time was still a senior player within the team. At the start of the year, he'd fallen out of favour with Ian Holloway and was sent out on a short-term loan to lower-league Fleetwood, where he suffered an injury his surgeon told him was career-ending. Regardless, he took the role as player-manager, and kitted up to play a couple of games when he thought it would help the team. Fearing relegation, and the financial impact it would bring, Oyston backed Ferguson in the market. It was mostly with stopgap loans and free transfers, but they were the targets Ferguson identified. He had an up-and-down relationship with Karl once he got the job, having rarely spoken to him before as a player. Ferguson claimed that one day they would have a productive chat and he would leave feeling supported, then the next day they would pass down the hallway and Karl wouldn't even acknowledge him.

Ferguson found it difficult to transition from a senior member in the dressing room – enjoying close relationships with most of the team and arranging nights out – to being the boss. He had even lived with several players over his time in Blackpool. Now he was responsible for naming and dropping them from the line-up. He tried to organise the team to be difficult to beat, which was the best way he thought they could scrap for survival. In his own words, 'We were shit to watch. We had to play a certain way. It was shit, but we kept them up.' He was able to keep the atmosphere within the dressing room relatively upbeat. Loan signing Andy Halliday went on to describe it as one of the happiest spells of his career, despite the poor results and toxicity all around them.

Blackpool sparked heavy media interest by bringing former protégé Freddy Adu in on trial, which was the best PR move the club had made for a long time. At 15 years old, Adu was described as the 'next Pelé,' but the world had watched with a twisted bemusement as his career continued to falter. Each step he took was followed with great interest. At 24, he was without a club and had become *the* cautionary tale for overhyping a young talent, and how development could go wrong. Adu joined training and couldn't get up to speed. Blackpool decided against offering him a contract, but he still stuck around for four months. The manager and team loved his attitude, and he was happy to stay. He loved being in the town, especially the nights out on a weekend.

One of the big problems Ferguson faced was the state of the Bloomfield Road pitch. It started cutting up badly the previous season and had deteriorated to such a degree that it was becoming unsafe to play on. It created constant headlines, as each visiting team would comment on how dangerous it was. Hull manager Steve Bruce blasted it to the press, 'The pitch was terrible, an absolute quagmire … People pay good money to watch good football but the pitch is so slow and horrible, it's a mess. It was difficult to move the ball and impossible to run with it.' After another game, with the pitch at its worst point, Nottingham Forest player Eric Lichaj commented, 'I don't think I've ever been part of a game like this one. For one, the pitch wasn't very good for us to play our usual game. I've never played on anything like this in my life. I didn't want to pass it back because it was really risky and the ball was bobbling up on our knees at times.' One journalist remarked, 'The lads playing football in World War I had a better surface than this.'

Ferguson had to wait nine games to get his first win. With each poor result, looking at the league table became a more and more nervous exercise. Slipping into the relegation zone seemed a mere inevitability. Blackpool Supporters' Association decided to write an open letter to the players, hoping to give them some motivation for the last few games. The chair of BSA was Glenn Bowley, who had numerous phone conversations with Ferguson and was impressed by how much the caretaker manager cared, and how much he wanted to put things right. He got the thumbs up to deliver the letter to the players. Many had joined on short-term deals or loans from other clubs. There were questions over whether their desire and commitment matched that of previous teams who had lined up in the tangerine shirt. The letter aimed to express the passion of the fans, to show how important the team was for them. The club might have been in a toxic state, but the fans were still desperate to avoid relegation. What Bowley didn't know was the spectacle which would surround the letter.

The club had the media department set up cameras, and they filmed captain Gary MacKenzie reading the letter to the rest of the players. They had all been hauled into the stadium that morning to attend the meeting. None looked particularly pleased with the sideshow. Local journalists were invited and BBC commentator Ian Chisnall held awkward interviews with players which, for some inexplicable reason, were uploaded to the club's official YouTube account. The whole process was heavily criticised by other Blackpool fans, who saw it as patronising and humiliating. Despite the underwhelming reaction, three senior players called Glenn Bowley the night before the next game to show their support.

Whatever the letter hoped to achieve, it didn't have an immediate effect as Blackpool went out in the next game and lost 2-0 to Leeds. Then came a night match at home to Derby. By now, fans had started organising protests against the Oystons, voicing their anger at the prolonged spell of failure. There had been a game where fans held up a fake £90m note from their seats, questioning where the money was going. In the second half against Derby, a large group of fans moved in unison from their seats, congregating right underneath the directors' box where Karl Oyston sat. This felt more spontaneous. It felt like something could spill over, like it wasn't a football game any more. At the directors' box, the group let fly with anti-Oyston songs and jeers. Also sat in the stands was a player from the Netherlands, Tom Beugelsdijk, who was about to sign for the club. After watching the demonstration, he got the first taxi to the airport and left, never to be heard from again.

Before the game, a fan had designed and printed a large banner which showed a cartoon image of a cow, filled with pound signs, that read 'Blackpool FC – Oyston's Cash Cow'. He was driving around town before the match with it on the back of his car, as a sort of mobile advertisement, unsure of where to park it. He decided to leave it right outside the club hotel and stadium, so everybody would walk past it on their way to the game. Before kick-off, Sam Oyston tweeted a picture of Karl posing next to the sign, with a big grin on his face, captioned, 'Karl loving the latest attempts to get him to spend money.' It was a predictable own goal, causing uproar among the Blackpool community. It spurred on those who were planning to protest and pushed others who were in two minds over the edge. Karl appeared on a local radio station and deflected blame on to his son for posting the picture online, rather than accepting responsibility for actually posing next to it. 'Sam is grounded and has had his pocket money stopped,' he joked.

Throughout the entire saga, with much more ire and toxicity to come, Karl would continually try to laugh off and belittle fan action. At one point he called the protests a 'busted flush', as they eventually turned into a boycotting campaign labelled 'NAPM', or 'Not A Penny More'. But in Sam's own reflections now, he admitted they were slow to react to how genuine the anger of the fans was. There had always been 'Oyston out' sentiment, lasting decades. It had become almost an in-joke at one point, especially as the club started climbing up the leagues, eventually getting to the very top. But it wasn't a joke any more, it was real. It was heartfelt. And it continued to escalate, further and further into an all-out war.

A group of fans had dubbed themselves the Tangerine Knights, with the aim of taking more direct action against the Oystons. By now, many supporters wanted to mobilise their anger and distrust over the way the club was being run. The Knights were determined to hold the biggest protest yet for an upcoming game against Lancashire rivals Burnley, being shown live on TV. There were four games left and

Blackpool were only just keeping their heads above water, two points clear of the relegation zone. The starting XI for the match was unrecognisable compared to the team that had been gracing the pitch under Holloway just a couple of years ago, playing scintillating, entertaining football. There were no wingers, and a journeyman defensive midfielder playing as second striker behind the only real forward on the pitch – who was subbed off 56 minutes in, with the team 1-0 down. His replacement was a 22-year-old product of the youth team who hadn't played a single league game in his career, and never appeared for Blackpool again. There were some hand-wringers who complained that protests would distract the team from performing on the pitch, but such a team had no chance of competing, and the confusing line-up choice from Ferguson handcuffed them more than any demonstration ever could. They lost 1-0.

The Knights helped organise a tennis ball protest, inspired by a similar demonstration from a game in Spain. They put their own spin on things, adding tangerines into the mix. In the 53rd minute a large group of fans threw over 200 balls and tangerines on the pitch, forcing a disruption in play. It could have been more, but the club's safety officer had gotten wind before the game, having infiltrated a private Facebook group where all the discussions were taking place. He later informed one of the organisers they might have gotten 1,000 on the pitch had the stewards not been tipped off.

As fans were entering the ground, stewards were conducting searches. Some managed to sneak through with tennis balls and tangerines stored down in their underwear. Women hid them in handbags. Others were less fortunate and loose tennis balls could be seen rolling down past the queue of people as they shook loose from their hiding place. In the South Stand was the Seasiders bar, where fans could drink pre-game. It was accessible from the stand at half-time but pre-game the doors were closed, and fans were forced to leave via the front entrance to go through the proper turnstiles. For that reason, there were no security checks at the bar pre-game. A group of Knights walked in, armed with bags full of tennis balls and tangerines, and stashed them in the ceiling of the toilets. Then, at half-time, they were able to walk back down from the stand and collect them.

The protest worked, interrupting the game for a few minutes as players and stewards had to individually pick up the tennis balls and tangerines and hurl them off the pitch, to a chorus of 'Oyston out!' songs from the fans. And it all played out live on TV for the whole world to see. It was totally unique for British football. The Oystons were, as ever, determined to show they weren't rattled. After the match a picture surfaced online of Karl's other son George, only in his early teens, posing for a picture in the directors' box with a big grin on his face, holding a tennis racket. At every turn the Oyston family were pushing Blackpool fans together. Karl had gotten a new licence plate for his Land Rover, which read 'OY51 OUT', which he parked on display outside the ground for fans to walk past. It was getting harder to ignore their actions, even for the most staunchly non-political supporter.

The manic scene of the protest was nearly one-upped by the actions of the Blackpool bench. Late in the game Stephen Dobbie, who had returned to the club on loan, was preparing to come on as a substitute. For some reason Bob Malcolm, Ferguson's number two, was unhappy with him. Whether it was because he was taking too long putting his shirt on, or for some other dispute, Malcolm exploded. The Sky cameras cut to the dugout and showed Malcolm squaring up to Dobbie. He pushed his head into Dobbie's, appearing to strike him at least partially with his hand, and had to be pulled away by the fourth official. It was a disgraceful scene. Malcolm was sent off by the referee and banished to the stands for fighting his own player, while Dobbie had a baffled look on his face throughout. It perfectly typified the inner war threatening to tear the club apart. Back in the dressing room after the game, players let loose in frustration. It was the culmination of months of losing, of constant failure, and led to an explosion of anger. Matt Gilks, the longest-tenured player, had been through it all. He pointed around the room to the players, telling them, 'You're fucking shit, and you're fucking shit!' Then he directed his ire at Ferguson, adding, 'And your training is fucking shit!'

There were three games left in the season. Despite whatever turmoil there might have been inside the squad, Blackpool were able to pick up a vital four points with a draw away at Brighton followed by a win at Wigan. Maybe getting their feelings off their chests had helped, and the results were enough to secure survival. In the best decision he'd made for a while, and last he would make for a long time to come, Karl had the club pay for the tickets of the 3,000 fans who travelled to the DW Stadium in an attempt to 'turn Wigan tangerine'. Blackpool started the day in the relegation zone but pulled off an impressive victory with roaring fans behind them. It would be the last time for many years the team would enjoy such support. On the final day Blackpool lost 3-0 to Charlton, but other results went their way and they finished the season inches above the relegation zone. The looming disaster had been averted, but without drastic changes from the very top, it was still beckoning.

Chapter 4

Protest & Libel

ON A gloomy, rainy Wednesday night before the start of the 2013/14 season, Tim Fielding left the office late. He worked as a solicitor just off Blackpool's famous Golden Mile. He made the short walk over to Bloomfield Road. He knew every step. He'd made that same walk many times over the years, but this time he wasn't going to the stadium. He walked right past it, instead stopping outside the neighbouring Number 1 club. Fielding stood at the entrance, waiting for somebody to come down and open the doors for the evening. The pub was hosting a meeting of a new supporters' group, Seasiders Independent Supporters' Association (SISA). It was formed when a handful of fans became disillusioned with the official fan group, BSA, and its perceived cosy relationship with the club. They wanted a new voice.

SISA didn't promote itself as a protest group, although there was an ingrained distrust of the Oystons and the direction they were taking the club in. The movement gained quick support, but not everyone was converted easily. Blackpool were only recently out of the Premier League, and fans sounding the alarm bell were at times met with ridicule for their negativity. Flyers and leaflets were passed around covertly in concourses and hidden into coat pockets, as if it were an invitation to a secret society. Plenty more were left on the floor, torn to pieces. As things continued to deteriorate on the pitch, numbers soared.

Fielding hadn't wanted much responsibility when he joined, he was already busy juggling his day job with coaching youth football. But his thoughtful manner and eloquence speaking to a crowd thrust him to the top of the group. As he waited outside, he saw Karl Oyston and Glenn Bowley, chair of BSA, walk over together from the stadium. When they arrived, they made a point to ignore Fielding. Instead, the two shared small talk between themselves. When the doors opened, Tim offered to buy them a drink, but they turned him down. 'We'll stay on our own,' Karl said. As the meeting began, Oyston and Bowley were sat at the back, giggling together, texting on their phones.

The group at this point could boast of regular meetings with well over 100 people showing up, but that night's particular gathering was sparsely attended. Only ten people were there. The meeting proceeded to item five on the agenda, ironically labelled 'Communication between SISA, BFC and BSA'. Considering the heads of all organisations were currently in a room together, an attendee tried to cut through the silliness. He asked Karl to address the small crowd. After a small, pleasant-enough speech, Karl delivered the only line he would tell them throughout the rest of the saga. There would be no dialogue, you are wasting your time. He repeated a message he'd said previously, directly to Tim Fielding, 'Go away and start your own supporters' trust.'

BSA had once tried to form into a trust, but fell at the first hurdle by not being independent. Trusts are formal organisations with financial accounts, registered members and constitutions. Karl didn't think they could pull it off, but he underestimated the people in the room that day. SISA's numbers swelled as Blackpool continued to nosedive. A year later, 1,000 people had joined up and SISA overtook BSA as the largest fan group. They passed a resolution by almost unanimous consent to form a trust, and Blackpool Supporters' Trust (BST) was born. Despite representing the largest body of fans, neither Karl Oyston nor anybody inside the stadium ever recognised them or engaged in dialogue. The reason he gave, and has repeated ever since, was that it was due to a commitment he made to BSA in the early 2000s. Back then they had been known as BISA, with the 'I' standing for 'Independent', but Karl had convinced them to drop that part of their name and work with the club. In exchange, he had promised to keep their relationship exclusive and recognise only their organisation as the voice of the fans. However, Glenn Bowley – who wasn't with BSA at the time of the agreement but was now in the top role – said he didn't recall having any conversations with Karl about the matter and expressed regret that he hadn't pushed him to recognise BST. There was certainly no suggestion that BSA was standing in his way, and Bowley clarified 'I wasn't overly bothered who he spoke to.'

Correspondence from BST was cordial and diplomatic. It was motivated only by wanting the best for the football club. But they were shut out. Undeterred, they achieved their aim of representing the fans and helped draw more and more attention to their plight. Fielding and future heads Steve Rowland and Christine Seddon pushed a media campaign to fill TV spots and column inches with the latest twists and turns at Bloomfield Road. Instead of BSA, now it was

BST who journalists would call for a quote. Membership continued to grow and an olive branch came from Latvia. Fielding secured a meeting with club president Valeri Belokon and his new director on the board, Kaspars Varpins, who replaced the departing Normunds Malnacs. They gained recognition from at least the minority shareholder of BFC. It was a vital relationship. Belokon was able to bounce ideas off Fielding and keep his finger on the pulse of the community. It helped inform his later legal action against the Oystons. He sent out open letters imploring them to put 'football first', borrowing a tagline used regularly by BST. It also helped Fielding work on attracting potential bidders for Blackpool, who might need to work with Valeri as a partner if they bought the Oystons out.

BST had more work to do on the home front. They were a driving force behind the 'Not A Penny More' campaign, encouraging fans to carry out an ethical boycott. They petitioned the Football League, pleading for any help they could get. All they received were generic statements offering little sympathy and even less help. Karl had been a member of the EFL board, and accusations abounded that they were making an internal decision to protect their own. In 2004, the EFL introduced a 'Fit and Proper Person' test in a lacklustre attempt at controlling who could own a football club. Their regulations stipulated that a person could not be involved in a team if they had a criminal conviction resulting in prison time of more than 12 months. It also disqualified anyone who had been on the sex offenders register. Owen Oyston fell afoul of both rules. However, Shaun Harvey, the CEO of the EFL, argued these rules couldn't apply retroactively. Since they had been introduced years after Owen's conviction in the 90s, he claimed there was little they could do. Fielding disagreed with the interpretation, and sought the advice of a barrister, who had dealt with significant sports cases before. He provided his opinion free of charge. He wrote that Oyston should be disbarred, using the words of the EFL against them from a meeting with BST, 'I confess that I find Mr Harvey's case as to why Mr Oyston does not fail the test to be incoherent. As Mr Harvey accepted at that meeting, "There is an annual re-certification."'

The EFL's position was essentially 'we are not a governing body', in effect admitting there was no oversight from a regulatory organisation. Without them, there was nobody else. Clubs could, by and large, do as they wished. It was later revealed that Owen Oyston failed the Premier League's own, separate test when Blackpool were promoted in 2010. This time, there was no ambiguity. The Premier League's own rules definitely did apply retrospectively. Richard Scudamore, the chief executive of the Premier League, wrote to the club demanding that Owen Oyston remove himself as owner. He suggested he transfer his shares to Karl instead. As with everything else that came out of the footballing bodies, even this threat was toothless and Owen refused to follow the order. It would seem Scudamore had either a lack of care or oversight in following up whether Oyston complied. Internally, Blackpool officials suspected the league were hoping they would get relegated before having to deal with it, which in the end is what happened. The Premier League saved itself a major headache and managed to brush the matter under the carpet.

BST and the fans behind them were on their own. So, they looked at other ways to isolate the Oystons and cut off their income streams. They communicated with businesses who had been sponsoring the club and implored them to pull their funding. Above all else, when Saturday after Saturday meant more demoralising losses on the pitch, they tried to prevent apathy. Apathy meant the Oystons could carry on as they wished. The fanbase needed to keep the pressure on wherever possible. Come wind, rain or shine, a group would turn up to every home game to picket, standing outside the main entrance in protest. They raised money for various causes with collection buckets, until the club stopped them. One Saturday they were holding a collection for Gary Parkinson, the ex-youth team coach who had suffered a stroke and still needed ongoing financial support. Stewards at the ground were instructed to stop the fans from collecting money for him on the premises. It was another needless act of cruelty which came out in the press and painted yet another black cloud over the club.

The fight against the Oystons was a two-pronged attack. The Tangerine Knights also stepped up, worrying less about taking a diplomatic route. The group prided itself on getting its hands dirty, taking action against the Oystons in their own back yard. The Knights were the agitprop wing of the two main fan groups, although both were smart enough to keep separated and not officially affiliated. They took cues from animal rights activists and other protesters who weren't afraid to push the boundaries of the law. Borrowing from the hacker group Anonymous, which for a time had the entire internet as captive audience to their exploits, they used Guy Fawkes masks and phrases such as 'Expect Us'. A group of around 30 travelled to Karl's house in a convoy of cars and coaches. They kept the plans secret until they arrived at the village down the road from his estate. There, they uploaded a picture posing next to the 'Welcome to Waddington' sign, all with their masks on, holding Tangerine Knights banners. Blackpool fans on social media were abuzz with excitement. It was a small symbol, but for the first time it felt like they were actually doing something; taking matters into their own hands and fighting back against the regime with collective action. While there were only a couple of dozen there, hundreds more felt involved by watching along online. They stopped off at a local pub and sat outside while planning their next move. That's when they saw Victoria, Karl's wife, drive past. Those there recall seeing her with a big, beaming smile on her face and say she started waving at them.

Nothing too dramatic happened at the event. Police arrived but there was never any real danger of violence. Members of the Knights explained they drew strict lines on their actions, not least because they recognised the importance of winning the PR battle. Fans set off smoke bombs and chanted every Oyston out song in the book. Police monitored the situation. They were on a public footpath that lay right next to the estate, and had a right to assemble. They dubbed it a 'ramble' trip, and the next one they organised properly, informing the police of their intentions beforehand and arriving in larger numbers. Then they went a third time, now with even more fans. It was a carnival atmosphere, dozens attended drinking beers, singing along. The rambles were as much about keeping spirits high and being together as they were about some far-off hope of getting rid of the Oystons.

While on the one hand decrying behaviour such as alleged death threats and abuse targeted at their small children, members of the Oyston family also seemed intent on giving as good as they got. Karl met protesters at the gates. Sam Oyston was seen smiling and taking pictures of the crowd. He'd already made himself a target through his postings on Twitter, where he regularly delved into abusive exchanges with fans rather than simply ignoring their attempts to provoke him – which he apologised for when asked for comment, describing himself as young and immature. Karl's wife went right up to the fans, screaming back and forth with the protesters. At one point someone flew a drone over the gate and into their field, hovering low to cause as much nuisance as possible. The Oystons had a small team of bodyguards in a car, who tried to ram it as it flew alongside them. But the speedy and nimble drone evaded their attempts with some fast flying from the operator. The scene was soundtracked by the fans cheerily singing the theme tune from *The Dam Busters*, letting out huge laughter and applause at each escape. A video circulated of Karl firing gunshots into the air as the crowd of fans had first arrived, walking up to his front gate. Some made complaints to the police on scene that he was trying to intimidate them. Karl held a firearms licence to shoot on his land and wasn't anywhere near the group. He denied he was trying to rile them up, rather clay pigeon shooting as planned for his daughter's birthday. Sam Oyston, however, said there had been some element of goading behind the shots.

As the Knights became more known, they got tip-offs from the enemies Karl had made of those once close to him. An ex-friend gave them the location of a Ferrari he used which he kept away from his properties. A family member even contacted them to give potentially compromising personal information. A smaller group in the Knights, of around four or five people, routinely arranged what they called 'coffee trips' – under-the-radar activities which were never made public and only a handful of people ever knew about. These included more trips to Karl's village, in the dead of night, where they threw around hundreds of propaganda leaflets about the family. They stapled them to trees, they taped them to fences, they threw them over garden walls. They wrote messages on the roads in big chalk writing, all hoping it would turn the neighbours against them and make them as hated as they were in Blackpool. They went to one of Owen's other properties, a lesser-known one which hadn't yet been targeted, and stole the front entrance sign. They kept it for over six months. Then on New Year's Eve they travelled back to Karl's house and left the sign on the front gate, spray-painted with the words 'Oyston Out'. It was an attempt at psychological warfare, just to let them know where they had been, that they were everywhere. The Oystons would, of course, profusely reject any suggestion it had the intended effect.

On another night, a small group brought along some 'banger ropes', ropes lined with small pyrotechnic explosives which farmers use to scare away birds. Once lit, they go off sequentially every 30 minutes. They set one off in a parking lot underneath a closed-down and abandoned building next to the stadium. Thanks to a large echo, an almighty bang went off after the fuse was lit. It was like a gunshot. All hell broke loose. Fire engines flew down to the scene thinking there had been an explosion. They left more at other Oyston properties. They had more audacious plans that never got off the ground, such as introducing moles on to the Bloomfield Road pitch to sabotage the playing surface. They had even consulted with a groundsman from another club who gave his opinion on the damage it would do. They looked into bugging 'Oyston Out' scarves that Karl had ordered, in his latest attempt to antagonise the group. Another idea was to go to Karl's house at night and build a temporary wall at his front gate, to stop his car being able to get out. More formal protests did go ahead frequently, with more fans involved. It was all in an attempt to keep momentum going and get into the newspapers, who gratefully covered the latest exploits in their filings.

What the Knights made no claim to orchestrating was the relentless campaign against Oystons Estate Agency, which had houses all along the Fylde coast. The company was set up by Owen Oyston in 2005. A year later Stuart Hall joined as a director. Hall was an ex-BBC presenter who was arrested in 2012 and pleaded guilty to 14 charges of indecent assault relating to 13 different girls aged between 9 and 17 years old. Many more women came forward with their own stories of sexual abuse and rape at his hands. On the very same day that Hall was appointed as a director, another also came aboard – William Roache, the actor famous for portraying Ken Barlow on *Coronation Street*. In 2013, Roache was charged under suspicion of raping a 13-year-old girl in 1967, but vehemently denied the allegation. He was vindicated in court as he was found innocent on all charges. His acquittal completely cleared his name, but for a period of time the estate agents had three directors on the board, all either convicted or accused of raping teenage girls. That was information certain people wanted to be made more public. On the company website every single property that was being sold was listed with the full address. Some fans mocked-up highly derogatory leaflets, then went to each and every door and posted them through the letterbox, letting the owners know just who they were using to sell their house. At the top was a picture of Hall, Roache and

Oyston all together, with the caption, 'Would you leave a friend or relative alone with these men? No, of course you wouldn't. So why trust them with your home?' Then at the bottom were the names and contact details of competitor estate agents in the area. It was unfair to Roache, who was innocent of the allegations, but after the leafleting the fans went back to the website and watched with joy the fruits of their labour. The list of 500 or so properties supposedly dwindled in half.

At the start of the 2015/16 season, the Knights themselves targeted the new shirt sponsor, a hotel chain called Village. One of their hotels included a golf course, so a small group sneaked their way on to the course at night and in spray paint wrote the word 'PILLAGE' in big letters on one of the greens. It angered plenty of people who thought they had gone too far, mostly golfers who thought the light graffiti was akin to sacrilege. But the CEO of Village, a football fan himself, immediately got in touch with the Knights to offer his help. He was horrified when he learnt what was happening at the club, professing his ignorance and admitting he'd not done his homework on the Oystons. He met with members from the Knights and BST and released a statement, promising to pull the sponsorship at the end of the season's contract. They couldn't withdraw from their current agreement, but didn't do any more promotional activities for the rest of the season. They even offered some of their facilities and meeting rooms free of charge for BST to use, going as far as supplying complimentary tea and sandwiches.

Owen Oyston needed a strategy. He wanted to shut the fans up. Not just the ones who were targeting his businesses, but anyone who was criticising him in the press and on social media. He turned to an archaic law that all too often protects the rich and powerful, and stifles the free and fair speech of everybody else. He wanted to punish the most vocal and scare dissenters into silence. In another shameful chapter in UK football history, the club started suing its own fans for alleged defamation. Alongside him was Karl, named as a joint claimant on each action. Those with knowledge of the situation are unanimous and adamant in saying Karl advised Owen not to go ahead with the plan, along with many others around him. Owen had his own group of people who worked for him, separate from the football club. While they worked to build the new business ventures he was trying to enter into, many tried to stay away from him. The door code at one of his properties was set to a specific key date from his prison days, such was their distaste at having to work for him.

Karl regarded the actions as weak and thin-skinned, and was at least smart enough to realise it would only feed the beast. It was a no-win situation. If they lost in court, it would be humiliating and cost money. If they won, they were targeting largely working-class people who didn't have much money to give them anyway, and it would only bring more scorn and hate on to their family. However, as Karl admits now, once the actions started he wasn't going to let them stop. He wouldn't let Owen get cold feet halfway through. In his view, to drop the claims after starting them would only make them look weak, and he wasn't going to let that happen. Although he portrays himself as merely playing a role as an 'attack dog' in the litigation, those who were sued all describe the actions of a man greatly enjoying doing so. As for Owen, a person close to him suggested the entire saga became a way for him to stay busy, 'He didn't actually have that much to do, but being the person he is, he's got no friends outside of work, he's got no hobbies. His hobby is sitting in the office scrawling paperwork, being busy, having meetings with people. "I'm so busy I've got all this legal work to do," but basically it's just his way of looking busy.'

Owen tasked his team, a group of advisors he'd worked with for many years, to trawl through message boards and social media to find anything he could sue for. Speaking now, Karl described it as a 'pathetic' exercise. They would spend hours each day reading every little comment. If they saw something – anything – they thought could be defamatory, they would print out the page and skip giddily into Owen's office to tell their boss the good work they had done. Owen led weekly update meetings on all the cases. Being the instigator of such legal action gave him an inherent advantage. He could send out letters threatening claims worth hundreds of thousands of pounds, and then bully people into taking the safe option to settle for a much smaller fee. It was how he was accused of operating in his business life. A 'bad payer', as described by his ex-wife Vicki, who could afford a costly claim where most others couldn't. As chairman of Blackpool Supporters' Trust, Tim Fielding was their biggest target. He was well known and well liked as a respected solicitor in the town. He was the first call when Sky Sports News or BBC Lancashire wanted to interview a fan. When he spoke, people listened.

Owen's team spent a long time searching through Fielding's posts. He was an active poster online over various BFC-related websites, but he was a solicitor after all, so he was cautious with his words. In the end they got him for nearly year-old posts, where he accused them of improper and potentially illegal financial activity in regard to payments out of Blackpool FC. Tim could have tried to defend his case, but the Oystons knew he wasn't going to. He was a partner in a law firm, and believed that if he lost it may have meant losing his licence to practice. It was a stressful and intense period, bringing many sleepless nights and a great deal of professional and personal worry. Fielding described it as like a 'headache that won't go away'. He agreed to settle.

He went into the stadium to meet with Karl. A telling demand was that he step down as chair of BST. They also wanted £10,000, which he hoped he could negotiate down. He'd been working closely with another fan who was being sued, Stephen Sharpe. Sharpe had met with Owen and managed to talk his proposed settlement figure down from £10,000 to £5,000. Tim asked if he could at least have the same, for parity. Except he wasn't asking Owen, who tended to adopt a softer approach in such meetings. Karl had made sure he was the one meeting with Tim directly. When Tim asked why he couldn't get his knocked down as Sharpe had, Karl replied, 'When you said anything people listened and it cost us a lot of money, he's just a dickhead.' Tim was a target because he was leading a contingent of voices against them. Sharpe, on the other hand, was just payback.

Sharpe had become a fairly prominent figure in the protests. He was banned from the stadium after the protest at home to Derby, when a group left their seats to march around the stands and congregate under the directors' box. Nevertheless, he carried on going to Bloomfield Road. At the tennis ball protest game against Burnley, he went right to the back of the stand underneath Owen's box and unleashed abuse directly at him. He put a target on his own back. By now they knew his name and face.

The last game of the 2013/14 season was at home to Charlton, and again Sharpe managed to get through the stewards and into the stands, but this time he was identified and kicked out. According to Sharpe, he was with his ten-year-old daughter when a group of stewards found him and surrounded him. They dragged him out of the stadium, leaving his daughter behind. Her grandad was in another stand and was able to collect her, but being separated from his child sparked a fury in Sharpe that he never let go. He was determined to do what he could to get back at the Oystons and get them out of the club. He knew a businessman who had plenty of money and encouraged him to buy them out. He brokered a meeting with the potential investor and Valeri Belokon in London, to talk about a potential future partnership.

Belokon was interested. His relationship with the Oystons had broken down since the Premier League season. He had pumped money into the club to get them to the top, and watched from outside the downfall as they took the profits. When the promotion windfall came, Belokon didn't want to cash in, he wanted to reinvest and compete. He generously reversed the profit-sharing deal from the Charlie Adam sale to benefit the club. He should have received 70 per cent, but instead he took 30 and left the rest in Blackpool to help buy new players. But he gave the Oystons too much credit. The money spent on the pitch was cut back year by year. By this point, he was already frozen out of decision-making. Both sides discussed buy-outs but were too far off one another on the price for negotiations to go anywhere. The impasse remained in place for several years and, busy with his other businesses, Belokon went quiet. With the club trapped in a death spiral, he started meeting with key fans and was kept briefed on what was happening on the ground. He began writing his open letters demanding change and he made occasional appearances in the local media repeating the same message. He started putting moves in place to find a resolution, preparing for a fight all the way up to the higher courts if needed.

Belokon's interest in buying the club only ever involved finding a local partner who could handle the day-to-day operations. His vision was to stay in Latvia and offer financial support from afar. In stepped Stephen Sharpe and his friend. During the meeting, Valeri expressed concern that Karl might be intercepting his letters to Owen. He still felt that the two shareholders could work something out, man to man, but Karl was in the way. He asked Sharpe if he knew how to get a letter directly to Owen, and Sharpe said he did, through his personal security guard. Belokon gave Sharpe the letter, sealed with a wax stamp from his bank, and Sharpe diligently sent it forward. Then, on a fans' forum, a mysterious username wrote to him, 'We know who you are, expect us to visit you.' Three days after he passed on Belokon's letter, he received his own papers. He was being sued by Owen, Karl and the football club. He had unintentionally made it known to them that he was working with Valeri. They wanted to take him out.

The alleged libel they were suing for was based around five posts he'd made on the same website. He sought legal advice and the solicitor assured him most were harmless. One called Owen a rapist, an offence for which he had been convicted for. Another called Karl a financial bully, the sort of milquetoast criticism shamefully picked up by the Oystons in their efforts to silence dissent. But there was one more that at least hinted at a threat, warning, 'You don't know what sort of war you are starting with the fans.' His solicitors sent letters back and forth with the Oystons and their team, costing Sharpe around £2,500. 'I can't keep paying this,' he thought. He decided to meet with them face to face to settle. During the meeting, Owen was playing good cop. He did the same with everyone. Karl had no such interest; he loved tearing a strip off people too much. Sharpe had to sit there and take it. 'This is why monkeys shouldn't use computers!' Karl shouted. He demanded £10,000. Owen and Karl left the room for a discussion in private. Owen presented their new offer, £5,000 if he paid within three days and published a grovelling apology.

After everything was settled, Owen bizarrely invited Sharpe to watch a game with him in the directors' box. 'Fuck off,' he thought, 'they just want to parade me around.' In almost every case, Owen was trying to stay friendly with the people he'd just sued. He did the same with Tim Fielding, offering him free tickets to sit with him. A person close to Owen remarked, 'He just wanted to be loved. He bought a football club because he wanted to be loved, he wanted to boost his profile. He didn't like people bad-mouthing him. He's gone through his whole life trying to be looked at as oh my god he's rich, he owns a football club, he's a property tycoon. He's driving a Rolls-Royce, wearing a ridiculous big hat and coat, all this image of being this top dog and schmoozing people.'

Sharpe had made one last post online which landed him in the most trouble. It was a reference to a particular story that was spreading like wildfire around the town and the fanbase. Some had noticed that several first-team players were missing games with no apparent injuries or other explanation. There was an air of mystery over why they were out of the team. Many players at the time were still staying at the hotel built into the stadium. Or if they weren't, they regularly socialised in the connected bar and restaurant. Above the hotel was a penthouse owned by Owen Oyston. Young women were seen to come and go on an almost daily occurrence. It was a source of embarrassment for many staff members. Owen's sex life was no secret, it was paraded for everyone to see. That was the point. One day, a fan called Frank Knight posted a story on his personal Facebook page – a story that many others were now passing around by word of mouth. It alleged that Owen had recently returned from a trip to Thailand, where he'd picked up a sexually transmitted disease. He then passed the STD on to a prostitute, who in turn passed the disease on to several players. The players then procured antibiotics from the club doctor, but either the drug itself or ingredients found in the drug were part of the FA's banned list of substances, and the reason the players were missing games was to avoid random drug tests.

The story was false. Those eagerly sharing it were blind to the holes in the accusation. It's not uncommon for rich, successful athletes in peak physical condition to have a sex life. It's not unheard of for football players to solicit sex. The odds are extremely high that over the years many footballers have caught sexually transmitted diseases. There is no medicine on the prohibited list of drugs, made publicly available each year, which would treat such a disease. The story leant on a xenophobic othering, that this was a particularly exotic disease because it was from a prostitute in Thailand. Above all else, it was libellous of Owen Oyston. He was furious at the story.

Except, as it turned out, there was *some* truth behind it. Some players had left the Blackpool hotel and refused to go back because they were uncomfortable with the atmosphere. There was no effective HR policy put in place to stop staff members getting close with players. It was an open secret that a young, but over-age, girl who worked in the waiting staff did have consensual sex with several players. She wasn't a prostitute, just a regular staff member. Some players did catch STDs and it is believed this was how it was passed. She was friendly with Owen, but it has been strongly denied by someone close to her that she ever had any sexual relationship with him. Every single source connected to the club who offered information on the subject flatly and strongly rejected the claim that any players missed games due to catching infections, and none believed Owen Oyston was involved. And neither was any evidence ever produced to suggest he was. Missing games certainly wasn't anything to do with the banned substance list. The anti-doping regulations state that 'testing may take place … at any time and at any location without advance notice.' Any suggestion of it being a disciplinary issue held little water either. Karl Oyston had seen all sorts in his years working in football, he certainly wasn't squeamish. His greatest detractors would say he cared about money and nothing else; jeopardising Blackpool's league status and subsequent income over what players did in their personal lives would be a highly improbable course of action.

Furthermore, the 'mysterious injuries' the players had weren't all that mysterious either. They were reported on at the time by the club's official Twitter account, in the *Blackpool Gazette*, and the manager spoke freely about them. They didn't all miss games at the same time and their length of absence varied, some only missed two or three games. The real story was no more scandalous than some footballers were having sex with the same girl and caught STDs. It had nothing to do with any missed games and there is no evidence Owen Oyston was involved.

So, while there was a kernel of truth, accepted by even those at the club, the rumour as it affected Owen was libellous. Somebody who saw Frank Knight's post passed it on to Owen and, as was his right, he immediately threatened a costly lawsuit. Knight, who was retired, had no appetite, and less still a defence, to attempt to fight back and risk losing the hundreds of thousands of pounds they were threatening to sue him for. He agreed a settlement for £20,000 and deleted his post.

When the news broke about what had happened, Blackpool fans immediately mobilised. Knight had been a fairly wealthy businessman, but in their eyes the Oystons had picked on a defenceless pensioner. Many other people by now were sharing the same story, and his post had only been seen by his 34 friends on Facebook, but unfortunately for him one of those friends also knew Owen Oyston. Joe Atherton, a well-known Blackpool fan, started a GoFundMe campaign and the £20,000 was quickly raised by fellow fans and returned to Knight. Celebrities such as Rachel Riley and Russell Brand shared the fundraiser on Twitter. A well-known actor donated £5,000 anonymously. The case only fuelled the bitter hate and anger towards the Oystons, bringing national attention and condemnation of their exploits.

The story had more victims still to come. It was shared eagerly by another fan, David Ragozzino. He went even further than the rest, falsely claiming it was 100 per cent true and that he could prove it. He challenged the Oystons to sue him for his posts. He was either reckless, fearless, or both. 'Raggy', as he was known, became an unlikely hero for some supporters – along with his friend Stephen Reed, who gave him legal advice. Reed had an extraordinary talent for getting under the skin of those he felt had wronged him, always quixotically fighting for some cause or another. A wiry, tall man with a big, greying bush of hair, he was affectionally given the nickname 'Afroman'. The two became regular faces at protests. Reed turned up to the Oystons Estate Agency office with a loudspeaker and made a Churchillian speech about how nobody in the town should work for such people. They both made rallying cries on message boards, calling the Oystons every name under the sun and dropping hints that more scandalous stories would soon come out. So far, Owen Oyston had targeted people who had something to lose. They ran a business or needed to protect their retirement savings. Ragozzino and Reed had nothing to lose. They were never going to go quietly into the night and surrender what little money they had. They became professional agitators.

When it came to what he'd actually posted, Ragozzino had a weak case. On top of sharing the false details of the STD story, he made the wholly false accusation that Karl 'had probably raped', either unaware or unbothered that the qualification of 'probably' did nothing to protect him from a claim of defamation. While they may have cheered them on, most reasonable people accepted Ragozzino and Reed had invited themselves to what came next, and they certainly didn't shy away from it. Together they declared a war they would fight through to the bitter end.

They were invited to Bloomfield Road for a mediation attempt. They made their way into the meeting room. There was a long table set out with two chairs laid out for them at one side, and then four for the Oyston team on the other end. The Oyston end had four bottles of water on the desk; none were supplied for Ragozzino and Reed. They were made to wait for 20 minutes. They decided to have some fun, taking selfies and posting them on social media for fans everywhere to see. They had absolutely no care or regard for how they were *supposed* to behave. They rearranged the table, swapping the chairs around and putting two of the water bottles in the bin and keeping the others for themselves. Raggy pulled out boxes of files and laid them out in front of him. There wasn't much substantial in there. 'It was just full of shit,' he explained. It was all part of the bluff. 'So how does this go then?' he asked the Oyston team when they arrived. 'Well, you need to make us an offer and we'll see if we accept before going to court.' 'Okay then,' Raggy replied. 'Give us £35,000 and we'll go away.' At that, Karl Oyston let out a bellowing laugh, cocking his head back in his chair. 'No, I'm being serious,' Raggy said. 'You took 20 grand off Frank Knight, ten grand off Tim Fielding and five grand off Steve Sharpe. Give us the 35 grand, we'll give it back to them, and we'll sign a piece of paper right now saying you'll never hear from us again.' Again, Karl burst out into hysterics; £35,000 going the other way might have done the trick. At that moment, Stephen Reed stood up. 'Right, that's it! I'm not dealing with you, you barcode tooth knobhead – Dave, I'm off. See you all in court!' The meeting ended.

Ragozzino and Reed continued their scorched earth campaign against the Oystons as they awaited the hearing date. But before it came, they were arrested for harassment. The charge referenced the masses of texts and emails they had sent several members of the Oyston family. This had become near 24/7 work for Ragozzino, targeting not only the Oystons but their associates and each member of their legal team. Emails flew out with titles such as 'Oyston the Nonce' and 'Was it because', an email sent to Karl's wife Victoria. It asked why he was banned from the stadium, listing 71 questions, each beginning with 'Was it because'. It included ridiculously daft questions such as 'Was it because you mistook Ragozzino for a new type of Italian Bolognese sauce?' all the way to threats such as 'Was it because I refuse to cease until the Oyston family are exterminated for crimes against society?' and everything in between. As the email progressed it got worse and worse, highlighting the particularly unfortunate way that some fans were weaponising rape accusations for fun. What had become lost was the 16-year-old victim of Owen's crime. Instead, Ragozzino was furiously typing things such as 'Was it because I enquired if any of the bridesmaids at your wedding had been victims of rape?' and throwing around quips about domestic violence as if they were trifling things to be laughed about.

The truth was that for nearly 20 years, few had really cared about Owen's conviction. Some had even believed him that it was all a conspiracy because of who he was, and that the girl was lying. The sudden emergence of hate and disgust was a convenient stick to beat him with. It should have existed from the very day it was made public, certainly when he was found guilty. Partially, however, it was an example of the 'Streisand Effect'. In notices of complaint, Owen alleged that calling him a rapist was defamatory. When word spread that he was suing fans for writing it, hundreds more joined in. As the cases earned more widespread coverage, supporters from other clubs were even discussing it on their message boards. Whenever the Oystons or Blackpool FC were mentioned, a post would quickly follow such as, 'Did you know Owen Oyston is a convicted rapist?'

The police were informed, which was the main reason Ragozzino and Reed were arrested for harassment. The email, admitted to even by the culprits, crossed the line. But Lancashire Police dropped the harassment case when they got hold of Karl's phone. They found thousands upon thousands of texts, going back and forth with 41 different fans, and concluded it was a two-sided affair. However, the damage for Ragozzino was already done. He had sent the email from his work account and it didn't take long for his office phone to ring. Karl was on the other end, laughing, 'You've fucked yourself now, haven't you?' Karl sent a letter to his manager, demanding an explanation as to why such an email had been sent from their offices. Ragozzino was fired.

He still wouldn't stop. Losing his job only made him more determined to fight, for now he had even less to lose. He claimed a group of heavyset men paid him a visit at two in the morning, pounding on his door. 'You leave the Oystons alone or you're a dead man,' they threatened. Karl laughed this accusation off and strongly denied it, offended more by the suggestion they would care enough about Ragozzino to do such a thing. If the Oystons ever did resort to such threats, they didn't need to. When the proceedings finally moved to court, the judge was scathing in his assessment. He awarded costs of £20,000 each to both Owen and Karl Oyston, and £1,000 to the football club. Not only did he find little difficulty in concluding the offending posts were libellous, he awarded aggravated damages because of Ragozzino's conduct. He was particularly damning of Reed, who sat in as an advisor in court. 'It is clear to me from reading this documentation and from observing Mr

Ragozzino and Mr Reed in court that he has not been at all well-served by the assistance of Mr Reed, since Mr Reed has been responsible for pouring yet more fuel on the flames rather than assisting Mr Ragozzino to present his defence with suitable moderation.'

The judge pointed to an order signed earlier in proceedings during settlement attempts, in which Ragozzino had consented to judgment being made against him, with costs to be decided later. Ragozzino claimed he was duped into signing the order, and that wording in the document had been added after the fact. The judge gave little credence to this uncorroborated claim. Part of his defence had already been struck out after he failed to fill in necessary documents the court required. Fans had followed along with the exploits for months, hoping he could pull a rabbit out of a hat. In the end, he was presented a bill for £41,000 plus costs, in a predictably one-sided judgment. Someone close to Owen advised him to put out a press release celebrating the victory and to magnanimously declare he wouldn't chase the money because clearing his name was the important thing. 'Are you fucking soft?' came his reply.

Ragozzino declared himself bankrupt and the debt was effectively wiped clean. Before that, though, he was hauled in front of another judge to declare his assets. Throughout the process he'd been trying to wind the Oyston side up, claiming to be richer than he was. He boasted of owning an expensive house and sent an email with a picture of himself posing next to one he happened to walk by one day. He claimed to have a fishing boat and set of luxury golf clubs worth a small fortune. With an Oyston aide sitting in, the judge asked him about the boat and golf clubs. At one point he asked how many microwaves he owned. Raggy couldn't even remember what that could be in reference to. 'Did I pretend I owned a microwave empire?' he chuckled to himself. The judge declared that he was, in fact, asset-less. He rented his house and he had not come into the large inheritance he once bragged about. He was able to make good on the one promise he continued to make throughout. He never paid the Oystons a single penny. It's hard to see how anybody came out of the situation better off.

Chapter 5

Retribution

'I'M GOING to bankrupt you. I'm going to leave you with nothing left.'

When Paul Crashley arrived at Bloomfield Road for his mediation meeting with Karl Oyston, he knew what to expect. Oyston and his lawyers would try to pressure him into signing something right then and there, to tie him into something later. They would hold the meeting in a room with one door and put him at the end of a table as far away from that door as possible, making sure he couldn't leave without walking past them first. But before all that, they'd make him wait.

They made him wait for 29 minutes. He knows it was exactly 29 minutes because he'd told himself he would walk at 30, to show them he wasn't going to be so easily pushed around. In the waiting area outside, Paul was kept company by Karl Oyston's youngest son George, still in his early teens at that time, sat in the corner texting and swiping on his phone. Paul was well aware of who George was – he would go on to find Paul's daughter and send her a friend request on Facebook. He was nervous, but his tensions eased when multiple members of staff came up to him and quietly wished him good luck. Even in their own building, the Oystons were hated. 'I hope you stick it to them,' one member of staff said, shaking Paul's hand.

Eventually, Paul was invited into the boardroom. They were there to talk about Paul's website, Back Henry Street, a fans' forum he ran voluntarily. A few months earlier he'd received notice that Owen and Karl were demanding he hand over his users' private details so they could sue them for defamation. Paul refused. He wasn't feeling particularly charitable, and without a court order he feared it would break data protection law. There were around a dozen posts on the website, from several different users, which the Oyston legal team had flagged as allegedly defamatory. The matter could go away with a simple deletion of the posts, which was likely what the goal was – to whitewash the message boards of comments about them they didn't like and make everybody think twice about what they said next time.

In an oversight, the posts weren't deleted in the necessary timeframe. As site owner he was now potentially liable for what other people had written. When the Oystons' team got in touch, he was already in a legal dispute over parental control of his teenage daughter, which he won. He was also dealing with a close family member seriously ill in hospital. 'At the time, the petty little grievances of the Oystons didn't seem important,' he said. He also failed to take the threat as seriously as he needed to. Someone claiming to be representing the Oystons had made a notice of complaint around 18 months previously, before anyone else had been targeted. Before Paul could respond, the posters had already deleted the concerning comments and nothing further came of it. When the latest notice of complaint came it was still late 2014, and the actions against other fans were not yet publicly known. A football club actually suing its own fans was almost unheard of.

The dilapidated facilities at the Bloomfield Road stadium offered little to be impressed about. It was full of rusted metal, the stands filled with ugly, faded salmon pink seats because they were painted in the wrong colour. Offices inside the stadium once flooded with rainwater, causing thousands of pounds worth of damage to computer equipment. The concrete in the stands hadn't been sealed properly, causing rain to fall through. The guttering needed to be cleared once a year, but it had been left to pile up and eventually caused a blockage. There was a problem with the small mountains of pigeon poo also piling up. It was discovered that Karl had been shooting pigeons at the stadium, and Sam Oyston tweeted a picture of himself sat in the stands posing with a gun, with a caption boasting he was doing the same. Local residents complained to the council, but it was found they had license to do it. Culling of pigeons is only allowed if they represent a health and safety risk, which the club said they did due to fouling where people ate and drank. On another occasion there was significant water damage to the sponsors' lounge and private boxes. The original plans for the new stands included a walkway to be used for maintenance, with easy access to the floodlights. Karl had cut the walkway from the plans to save money. If he hadn't, it would have helped collect puddles of rain which instead fell on to the facilities below.

The only grandeur the stadium held was saved for the boardroom. The inside was all oak-panelled, with the panels lifted from Admiral Lord Nelson's flagship HMS *Foudroyant*, which had been wrecked on Blackpool beach. In the office was a large rectangular table. As Paul walked into his mediation meeting, he was shown to a seat at one end of the table. Karl and his lawyers were at the other. They made sure to place Paul away from the door, just as he thought they would.

The comments on the message board ranged from clearly problematic to the downright uninteresting. There were unsubstantiated allegations of criminal activity, albeit made off the cuff with little realistic prospect of ever being taken seriously. Other posts should have been seen as uncontroversial venting of frustrations, but the Oystons jumped on criticism such as comments which labelled them 'thieves' and 'conmen' and argued they were meant literally, choosing to ignore the more common, colloquial meaning. It was the sort of criticism that Crashley felt ought to be protected as 'pub talk', fair complaints any fan would have, shared in pubs and around dinner tables across Blackpool.

Another poster simply listed transactions the Oystons had carried out, information lifted from the club's own financial accounts. He mentioned Owen's £11m payment and the many more millions loaned to other Oyston-owned companies, all interest-free and unsecured. It was an objective, provable fact, yet they tried to sue him. They claimed that comments such as 'the club is finished', or 'the Oystons are parasites' were defamatory. Another post wrote that what the Oystons were doing was so bad, 'it's criminal'. It was the most heinous example of their contortion, stretching a word's common definition beyond its breaking point. The comment had been written by a fan called Gerald Mortensen. Mortensen lived in Wisconsin, USA. He had never even been to Blackpool. He had no reason whatsoever to care about a town in the north of England and its football team. But he got hooked in their sole season in the Premier League. He woke up early on his weekend mornings to follow games – not even to watch, because most weren't televised, but to listen to a live commentary stream that would often stop working midway through the game. He wasn't doing this for Manchester United or Liverpool, but for Blackpool. For all this, the Oystons tried to sue him because he decried the downfall of the club by saying 'it's criminal'. Once they added their by now routine request for aggravated damages, the claim against Crashley was for £150,000.

Paul had been able to hire a solicitor for a few weeks, thanks to a donation fund that raised around £2,000. Regular users of the website all chipped in, as did rival Preston fans. The story went worldwide. He had donations from Russia, Australia and America, where a woman said she had read about his case in the *New York Times* and was so disgusted she immediately went online to give money. His solicitor had emailed their terms before the meeting. Crashley would give a full apology, take the site down, and make a small payment of around £300, the amount left over in the donation kitty. At the meeting, money wasn't mentioned. The two sides spoke about taking the site down and a formal apology. At this point, Paul was steadfast in sticking to his one golden rule, given to him by his mother who had worked on employment tribunals for years. *Don't. Sign. Anything.* He asked for the weekend to think about it, and then the theatrics ensued.

He tried to explain that the point of the meeting had been to start discussions and then take more time to consider any proposals. 'No it wasn't!' Karl erupted, 'It was for you to persuade us not to make you bankrupt and end up with this website anyway. Which is what's gonna happen, and that's what I'm inclined to do! We'll find out what you've got and what you own when you go bankrupt. We'll get exactly what you've got. So don't think you're sitting there in some strong position because you're not!' Karl eventually stormed off. He stood up, shook Paul's hand, and walked out of the boardroom, but not before giving one last remark. 'Good luck,' he said, 'You're going to need it.' This was going all the way to court. Paul had a fight on his hands.

Over the coming months, progress in the case stalled. The court date got pushed back several times. The delays only added to Paul's distress. He faced agonising waits for the latest update and started suffering from depression, followed by a bout of insomnia. At first, he struggled to sleep because of the panic and fear of what might happen. Then, as he started to gain confidence that he could win, it was because of a lightbulb moment at 1am that had him up the rest of the night googling case law. While they were waiting for a judge to decide a date, the Oystons made a new settlement offer. They wanted £20,000. 'Well I haven't got 20 grand, so I might as well go to court,' Paul thought. They also wanted him to agree to never build another website that could be used to defame the Oystons. Paul was a web designer by trade, building websites was how he made a living. It was far too vague for him to agree to the stipulation.

Eventually, Crashley decided he had to quit his job. Coming home after a long day at work to research and write his own defence was too much to handle. He cobbled together enough money to see a therapist to help him through it, but ran out of funds after three months and had to stop. 'It was hard to describe. Just very dark. I couldn't concentrate on everything. My mind was continually racing.

Every single little thing, it was like a chain reaction. I'd think of something then it would split off into five different things and I'd think about all of them. To the point of physically, I could feel it in my head. It was very strange. I was never suicidal, but I was definitely incapacitated and also completely unable to sleep.' He calculated he had worked on his case for 930 hours. His girlfriend laughed off the suggestion – it was way more than that.

Despite the stressful delays, Paul had confidence in his defence. His expertise in building websites gave him an advantage. Where the Oystons and their legal team tried to point to page views as evidence of how many people saw the posts, he was able to correct them and point out these did not count as unique users, more likely being the same handful of people refreshing the page several times. Further, he looked on in bemusement at evidence they sent over which only included screenshots of 4 of the 6 posts, leading him to believe they had failed to save copies of the others. They provided no screenshots of any posts still existing in the weeks after the initial complaint, a vital part of their claim.

What Crashley didn't know at the time was that a lawyer who had at one point worked with the Oystons on other cases was actually going behind their back to help him. The lawyer had been in contact with a moderator on the forum and had written a letter for Paul to send to Owen Oyston, which set out a reasonable and polite case for the action to be dropped and for all sides to walk away from the mess. Other advisors were more overt, continuing in ill-fated pleas to get him to drop the existing cases. The letter didn't work, but it didn't matter. The Oystons had forgotten to pay an important court fee in time, basically resulting in a loss by default. The judge struck out the claim and awarded costs in Crashley's favour. Speaking now, Karl admitted the whole case was a 'dog's dinner'.

Karl tried to suggest to the media they had dropped the case in an act of their own mercy, but it was all scrambled out a little too late. Paul was sitting on a letter of confirmation and waited until a day when the Oystons were in court over another action, and at that moment sent out the celebratory post on the forum to announce he had won. In doing so, he gave himself a few hours to get ahead of whatever spin they could attempt. If it *was* true they had dropped the complaint out of a newly found sense of compassion, Owen Oyston certainly didn't know anything about it. The group of fans being sued had become quite close, working together to share ideas and vent frustrations. Stephen Sharpe was one of those people. He bumped into Les Goulding, Owen's private investigator, while holding a copy of the *Blackpool Gazette*. Goulding had become infamous among the Blackpool community of fans, as he was always the one tasked with serving papers. His presence became a harbinger of doom. The front cover of the *Gazette* featured Paul's story, detailing how he'd won his case. Goulding hadn't read it, and apparently neither had Owen. 'How is Paul doing?' Goulding asked. 'Well, he's chuffed, obviously,' Sharpe replied. But Goulding still didn't understand. 'So, Owen is wondering when he will take the site down? Will he be all right, will he be able to pay?' Sharpe showed him the newspaper. It was only then that Goulding realised the Oystons had lost. They had to pay Paul money. 'Oh,' he said. 'Owen's not going to be happy about that.'

The tide was turning. After some early concessions, the Oystons suddenly found the litigation was no longer going their way. A Blackpool fan decided to seek his own revenge. It was February 2014, and Blackpool had just lost 2-1 to Birmingham, marking 15 games in a row without a win. While everyone else was venting their anger on social media, Sam Oyston was having fun. He got involved in an argument with a fan called Andy Grice, who had worked at a casino neighbouring the stadium and had thus far had a pleasant enough relationship with the club and the Oystons, who frequented semi-regularly. Sam tweeted at him, 'How come you left the casino? Or is it a touchy subject? #stickyfingers'. It was an unfounded allegation of theft, and Grice knew he had him. Sam alleged Grice had been sending abuse on social media directed at the club hotel, taking photos of an empty car park and claiming nobody ever wanted to go in. As the manager, he took it personally, so he clumsily replied with the allegation and arrogantly refused to retract. It was time for some retribution, and one of the Oystons was finally going to have to apologise, in public, to a Blackpool fan.

At first that's all Grice demanded – a public apology. But Sam refused. He challenged Grice to leave it to the lawyers, declaring he would never apologise. Grice had a decision to make. He didn't have property or assets, he had nothing to lose, and he knew how sweet it would taste for a Blackpool fan to finally have their day in court. So, he left it to the lawyers. He received a letter which claimed Sam had obtained evidence of him stealing from the casino, along with a threat of retaliatory action over tweets Grice had made at the Football League official account. He had written 'what about the millions of pounds taken out of the game? What about our community?' which the Oystons apparently took offence to – even though the tens of millions flowing out of Blackpool FC was a provable, objective truth, volunteered by their own accounts. Another tweet, again aimed at the Football League, went 'You have to be implicated in the cover up that is seeing Blackpool FC die.' Grice was wise not to take these threats too seriously, as it would have been an exceptionally weak case for libel. He was, however, far more furious at the mention of a separate, unrelated workplace dispute that Sam Oyston had clearly heard about, and was using in an attempt at pressuring him to drop the claim. He questioned how such information could have gotten into their hands, and threw back counter-accusations that it was a breach of data protection.

Then, with his court date nearing, he got a call from his lawyer. Sam was sat in his office, ready to make a deal. The offer was £20,000 and an apology. The apology went up on a popular fans' forum called A View From The Tower (AVFTT). It received thousands of replies from Blackpool fans, basking in the humiliation. Every time it slipped down the main page it was bumped to the top all over again.

Grice's card was marked. The Oystons wanted to get back at him, looking to find something they could sue for. Grice had to be extremely cautious and diligent, but he slipped up. On a post to the same forum, he wrongly described one of the Oyston legal team, Graham Woodward, as 'struck off'. It was a fateful error. Woodward was a practising solicitor and wasn't struck off; this was a highly defamatory allegation against a solicitor with an unblemished record. The name he meant to say was Jim Rawlinson, Owen's other advisor, who had indeed been struck off. Throughout all the cases against fans, Rawlinson was described as being heavily involved, even though his criminal conviction for fraud placed heavy limits on what he could do. They seized on it. The paperwork started and Grice noticed Les Goulding following him around. He knew straight away it wasn't going to end well for him. At a mediation meeting, Woodward asked for a settlement of ten grand. 'Ten fucking pence?' Grice responded, laughing incredulously. He didn't have ten grand to give. Of the money he'd been awarded from Sam, only three went into his pocket after court and legal fees. 'You think I'm going to give you ten grand? Fuck off, we'll go to court.' In the end, the judge decided Grice had to pay £18,000, but he had no intention of doing so.

The next morning, the phone rang. According to Grice, Karl Oyston was on the other end. 'What the fuck do you want?' he answered. 'Oh! A bit sore are we?' Karl said, laughing. 'Right, Andrew, I'll do you a deal. Pay us two grand and write a statement saying you will never talk about the Oystons again. Just fucking pay up like I told my son to.' When Grice declared he would never pay, he said Karl threatened they would chase him for the money. Karl denied he ever spoke to Grice, but if the call did happen, it was the last Grice ever heard from them. The money wasn't Karl's or Owen's to chase. He had been sued by Graham Woodward, but Woodward, to his credit, never came to collect his money.

If the Grice cases ended in a 1-1 draw, the case against Jeremy Smith could only have been described as a devastating loss. Smith had been a Blackpool fan all his life. In the 90s, the local car dealership he ran started sponsoring the club. For years he would sit in the sponsors' lounge, rubbing shoulders with the Oystons and putting money into the club. He was part of a table of ten who would go every week, enjoying the food and beer more than the lower-league football. Karl and Owen would come over to greet them.

They shared a drink every now and then and had some banter back and forth. Like every fan, he rode the wave as the team reached unthinkable new heights, and was dismayed and disgusted with the subsequent fall. He was deeply upset at how the Oystons were mismanaging the club. On the day of a home match against Cardiff in October 2014, fans were planning to walk out on the 53rd minute in protest. By now, Smith was sitting in the stands alongside them, he had moved down to take in the football properly. The *Blackpool Gazette* had featured a long interview that morning with Owen Oyston. He hit out at criticism and gave his rehearsed speech about how he'd saved the club. The front page was a large picture of his face, with the headline next to it reading 'We Are Not Thieves'. Before the game, Smith was browsing the message boards. He saw somebody post, 'Wouldn't it be funny if someone drew a line over the "Not"?' He borrowed the idea. The interview had stirred something within him. The charade of it all.

As he was leaving with the mass of fans in the 53rd minute, he held up a copy of that day's *Gazette*, featuring a heavy line of black ink which left the phrase 'We Are Thieves'. He was one of hundreds of fans protesting, but he didn't know what he'd just started. He hadn't taken his phone with him. When he got back home and checked it, he knew instantly. Everyone was texting him. People from all over the world had seen the match on TV and the moment the Sky cameras zoomed in on Smith, holding up the paper. That included the Oystons. A week later the papers came through, with a demand to pay £10,000 or face legal action. After he got past the initial sinking feeling, deep in his stomach, he was stirred with a resolve to fight back. 'I've got a chance to stick the knife into these bastards, they're just being cocky now, they think they can have anybody they want,' he thought.

Smith represented himself at an early date in court, a procedural day to set up what was to come. At the very end of the day, the judge leaned forward, looked him dead in the eye, and said, 'Mr Smith, I *strongly* suggest you get yourself a lawyer.' He left the court and walked straight to a local solicitors' office and had them take on the case. There was something in the judge's eyes, the way they locked with his. To him the message was clear, 'Get yourself some proper representation and you'll walk this.' Once he got a proper firm behind him, his confidence grew. He watched in disbelief as the other side sent through correspondence with misspelt words and typos. Even the word 'thieves', the single word the entire case boiled down to, was spelt 'theives'. He asked his barrister, 'How much is it going to cost to fight?' 'Well, how deep are your pockets?' came the reply. 'C'mon,' Smith asked, 'how much do I need?' 'Fifty grand. But if you lose, it could be up to half a million you pay out.' Smith thought it over a second. 'Does 50 grand get me in the ring with them?' The answer was yes. So, they got to work.

It didn't take long for their first win, delivered gift-wrapped from the other side. The claim was supposed to be from Owen, Karl, and Blackpool Football Club as the third claimant. They forgot to include the club in a document submitted to the court to start the claim. Smith watched on with satisfaction as the judge read out, 'I hereby strike Blackpool Football Club out of proceedings.' One down, two to go. Everything was progressing as expected, until four days before the main case hearing in Liverpool. Owen and Karl had amended their claim and were now asking for aggravated damages. They were seeking an eye-watering

£250,000. The day before the hearing, Smith's solicitor called him. He claimed to have found a hole in the Oystons' claim and knew a top QC in London who would come up to help. If Smith paid for him, that would significantly boost his odds of winning. 'Fucking hell,' Smith thought, 'how much does this cost now?' The QC was quoted at another £10,000, for one day's work. He was assured he would get it all back if he won, so he went for it.

They all arrived at court in the morning. Smith walked in with his team around him, his solicitor, barrister and QC all bringing up the rear. As he passed the court steps there was a bundle of Blackpool fans there, and even a small contingent of local Liverpool and Everton fans who wanted to show their support. They entered the building and his new QC took the barrister with him to meet the Oystons' team privately. They came back 15 minutes later and told Smith they had come to an agreement. 'Okay, they'll drop the case, it's all over. They'll pay your costs.' 'Just like that?' Smith asked. 'It's all over?' All that remained was for his lawyers to huddle together, and they totted up the total cost. The final bill that the Oystons had to swallow, for their case against Jeremy Smith for holding up a newspaper at a protest, was £180,000 plus interest.

The entire series of actions against fans was a misguided exercise, orchestrated by Owen Oyston but merrily carried out by Karl too. There had been abuse which any reasonably minded person could agree went too far, along with false and unfounded accusations, but most of what they sued for were pithy comments that hurt the feelings of a multi-millionaire who wanted to keep himself busy. In trying to vindicate their reputations, they inflicted pain, stress and financial woe on to some of the most diehard fans. A fan who only wanted to build a website where others could congregate and talk about their club. A fan who helped build the largest supporters' group around and gave up countless hours of his spare time to help. A fan who put thousands of pounds in sponsorship money into the club when they were stuck in lower-league purgatory. In the majority of their libel actions, they operated in the same manner they had run the football club and other businesses for decades, using bullying and threats to get their way. But ultimately, their tactics backfired. They lost a lot more money than they ever won. Along the way, they tarnished whatever was left of their reputation. Among football fans, the Oyston family name was infamous. But now they were known and despised all around the world. And they brought it all upon themselves.

Chapter 6

The Riga Revolution

THE SUMMER of 2014 was the last chance the Oystons had at getting fans back on board; £8m was still to come into the club from the Premier League parachute payments, the last of the promotion legacy. In a savvy business move the club froze the previous year's season ticket prices, which had already been set at a cut-price rate of £195.30, to celebrate 60 years since their famous FA Cup win. Many jumped on the promotional offer, which was a bargain price for what they hoped would at least be competitive Championship football. During the accelerating decline in the 2014/15 season, it artificially ensured that a minimum level of attendance was almost guaranteed. But before a ball was even kicked, fans were already demanding refunds. It was a summer of chaos, each disaster closely followed by another.

There exists no clear line marking the passing of old and new eras. It might have felt like longer, but it was still only three years since Blackpool had been playing in the Premier League. Some fans still hoped that by hiring the right manager, with some money to spend, they could climb back up the table. Paul Ince had taken a lot of the criticism; the systemic rot at the core of the club had not yet revealed itself fully. But it was coming. The skeleton crew of staff behind the scenes was stripped back even further. Club secretary Matt Williams departed for League Two Shrewsbury, where he earned a substantial pay increase. Without him, Karl Oyston now had few qualified people he could trust. He started the search for a new manager, passing up Barry Ferguson for consideration to take the role permanently. The backroom staff all departed and there was a mass exodus on the playing side, with most of the first team out of contract. All eyes turned towards who the new man in charge would be.

There was plenty of anxious expectation for Karl to make a splash with a manager with a proven track record in the division, who could turn the club around. With so much work required to build a new squad from scratch, urgency was needed. This anxiousness turned to frustration as the seven-to-ten-day timeframe Oyston publicly set out came and went. Thirty-seven days passed. On 11 June, José Riga was hired. Karl was quick to bat away criticism of the search, 'With what has gone before, we felt it was very important this time to do some real work to get the right man. We decided to see and speak to plenty of people and get as much advice as we possibly could. That's what we've done. It was important that we took our time. There's a bit of a fallacy that you should always do things quickly, but we decided to try to do things properly.'

It was an odd quote. It probably unintentionally admitted the unprofessional way he conducted searches in the past. His 'new' approach was impressive spin, considering the process he'd just undertaken. Before Riga, he interviewed Lechia Gdańsk manager Ricardo Moniz. In his delegation to Poland he invited under-18s manager Richie Kyle, Blackpool

Supporters' Association chair Glenn Bowley, and a local sports writer who happened to text him the night before asking if they had a new manager. The interview did not go well. Moniz knew little about Blackpool and Karl cut the meeting short. The search continued and Karl eventually met with Riga and his agent, Christopher Nathaniel, taking just Bowley with him this time. Riga had arrived in England only a few months earlier to take over at Charlton, who were 20th in the table with 30 games gone and only out of the relegation zone on goal difference. He immediately changed their fortunes, guiding them to safety with a seven-point cushion. When the *Blackpool Gazette* ran a poll asking fans who their preferred hire was, Riga easily won. Whatever biases and stereotyping such attitudes expose, he would be the first foreign manager in Blackpool's history. It inspired a certain level of excitement. He was handsome, wore well-fitted suits, and had worked in the youth set-up for AC Milan. It wasn't a hard sell when Blackpool's marketing team sent out their season ticket deal promotions under the headline 'Riga Revolution'.

Riga was equally as excited at the opportunity, for he had fallen in love with English football. He craved the intensity of the games and the feeling of a full stadium, where every minute of every game mattered so much to each supporter. For him there was nothing else like it. In his interview, he explained how he'd taught the players at Charlton to move away from a 'kick and rush' style of play to possession-based football. Most importantly, he'd done it while winning games with a young squad. Karl was impressed. He messaged Nathaniel afterwards to inform him he wanted to move forward.

The next step was a tour of the stadium and training ground, where Riga got his first surprise. 'Oh my God,' he thought to himself as he looked around the old, unfit infrastructure. The pitch was fine enough but that was about it. There wasn't much of an office for himself. The physio tables were falling apart and barely useable. The showers were a state, most didn't bother to use them and instead went back to the stadium to use the ones there. But Riga wasn't looking for luxury. He claimed Karl promised him he would make changes to bring the facility up to a better standard. That was all he needed to hear. 'Okay, let's go,' he said, and signed the contract. He was, in his own words, naïve. On the day he was introduced to the media, a local football writer recalled knowing immediately it wasn't going to work, 'The minute I saw him, the way he was talking, I thought this isn't Blackpool Football Club. I don't know what you've googled.' The warning signs were quick to show for Chris Nathaniel too. The negotiations had been eye-opening for him. It was his first time dealing with Oyston and he was beginning to see what type of man he was after the initial sales pitch, 'He didn't value human beings at all. He thought it was almost like master and servant, that's how he operated.'

It was a gargantuan task for Riga to get things ready for the new season. He was starting with a clean slate, taking over a squad with just six senior players. As ever, the onus fell completely on the manager to handle recruiting. There was no director of football or chief executive to help. There was no scouting network in place to quickly identify targets, and no youth prospects ready to kick on and jump up to the first team. Fans were expecting a flurry of new signings after the manager put pen to paper, but all they got was silence. Days passed. Weeks passed. Pre-season training was due to start on 1 July, but embarrassingly the club announced it would be delayed. They hadn't signed a single player. They didn't even have enough to play a five-a-side match together. At the end of the previous season, Blackpool had released a statement which declared they hoped to retain eight senior players who were out of contract. Only one agreed to come back. Matt Gilks, the last remaining member of the promotion team, refused to return when he was offered a pay cut via text. He'd played every single minute of the season in goal. With his departure there was nothing left of the legacy of the side that achieved the Premier League miracle. Ian Holloway had been correct in his assessment. Karl was going to cut the budget every year and give insulting offers to those who had achieved so much for the club.

With pre-season training delayed, Riga at least managed to assemble a backroom staff despite a limited budget. He added Bart De Roover as his assistant and Noel Blake as coach. Blake had been head coach of the England under-19 team for the last five years and Riga hoped he could help coax young English talent to join them. His plan failed, as he realised Blake didn't have as strong a connection with the players as he expected. They also struggled to sell Blackpool to players developed through elite academies in the Premier League. They were used to environments of extremely high levels of professionalism, with all the luxuries they could ask for. Blackpool offered nothing of the sort. It was a big part of Riga's vision that never made it off the ground.

The transfer stand-off started almost immediately, with José and Karl having different ideas of the calibre of player they wanted to bring in. Riga sifted through hundreds of potential targets, primarily using a scouting tool called Wyscout, which collects and organises player analytics and video. There, he could watch endless clips, such as all the individual player or team counter-attacks from a certain game. He looked at breakdowns of stats like average passing distance to decide who might suit his preferred style of play. Riga wanted Blackpool to return to the attractive approach they became famous for under Holloway. The players he did have were receptive to the idea. They wanted to play with the ball at their feet.

The amount of recruitment needed to build a squad, competitive or not, was overwhelming. Karl stressed the importance of José and the coaches meeting each player beforehand and judging their character. He wanted them put through a trial first, before making an offer. But Riga needed proven players, who had no reason to entertain a trial period. There was a method behind Oyston's thinking, it was just misguided. He wanted to get back to the way his previous managers had worked. Simon Grayson had a fantastic hit rate during his time at the club, building a team that got promoted from League One in 2007 and consolidated in the Championship. The core of the squad Holloway took to the Premier League were his signings. Grayson was insistent on doing lots of research about his potential additions, meeting them and judging how they would fit in his group. Oyston would be about to finalise a deal when Grayson would ring him at the 11th hour to call it off, 'Don't sign him! I've heard this story; I don't want him anywhere near us.' Unfortunately, such an attitude towards the transfer market was impractical when Blackpool needed to bring in over 20 new players in a matter of a few weeks. Even when Riga did arrange meetings with a player and his agent, on at least one occasion he alleged Oyston failed to show. It was a constant source of frustration for the manager. He found it difficult to reach Karl on the phone or by email, and rarely found him in his office, echoing sentiment from Michael Appleton. Karl shot the same accusation back at Riga.

Communication between the two collapsed from day one. In Karl's telling, José gave him a list of 11 players on his first day, then went to his hotel room and refused to come out until they were signed. In José's telling, he was using Wyscout to sort through hundreds of players and was exhausted and frustrated at the repeated knock-backs by Karl. 'You seem to work for nothing. For me, it was more a lack of communication and the personality of the chairman. I had no problem with anyone before. I'm not a conflictual guy, just let me do my job. Okay, you cannot give me this player, this other one will be perfect – even with less qualities but maybe with bigger motivation. I can make a squad of 25 players in one day. It takes five minutes. But that was not my objective.' Karl's targets were whoever was cheapest. Free agents sat around waiting for the phone to ring, who would join training without a contract if it boosted their chances of getting one. At one point, Nathaniel alleged Karl's son Sam was suggesting players that they should sign.

Out of Riga's priority list, he only got José Cubero, a Costa Rican holding midfielder who showed some flashes when he eventually played. Work permit issues meant he wasn't eligible until the ninth match of the season. As with all his dealings with the club and Karl, Riga could never get a straight answer as to what was happening. Each week he would call the new club secretary, Chris Hough, to ask if the permit was ready. Every time, he was told it would be ready the following week. Just like in the Premier League summer, Karl was enjoying the furore from outside over the lack of transfers. He bragged to Nathaniel one day, 'I love the fans hating me. I love it. The more they do it, the more it gets me going.' He showed him his 'OY51 OUT' car number plate, which he'd been given by a family member as a present. On 4 July, three weeks after Riga joined, the first signing of the summer arrived – Sergei Zenjov. The name still sends a shudder down any Blackpool fan's spine. An attacker, he was dubbed the 'fastest man in Estonia'. He played in eight games, scored no goals, and was released halfway through the season. But it was a new signing, finally. Then everything went quiet. Days and weeks passed, again.

On 15 July, Blackpool cancelled their upcoming training camp in Spain. They only had eight players. Instead, they made the trip down to Penrith to play a friendly. In a soon to become infamous tweet, the club account announced the matchday team: 'TEAM: Trialist, Waddington, Trialist, Perkins, McMahon, Dunne, Zenjov, Trialist, Trialist, Grant, Trialist.' The scattering of Blackpool fans who travelled down for the game made a point to give Riga rapturous applause. Riga hadn't spoken to the press since the day he'd joined six weeks earlier. He enforced a media blackout, refusing to do pre- or post-match interviews on the day of the game. But the fans were in his corner. Two days before the Penrith friendly, news had broken in the *Daily Mail* that Riga was about to quit due to the transfer stand-off. The backroom staff Riga assembled had yet to sign contracts and were working unpaid. The fans were relieved to see Riga show up to the game at all.

Internally, the relationship between Riga and Karl had broken down so quickly that the Belgian was nearly sacked before a ball was kicked. Each side blamed the other. Particularly, Karl accused Riga of identifying only UK-based targets in his job interview, then switching to exclusively foreign targets once he arrived. This claim was refuted by Riga, Chris Nathaniel and Glenn Bowley – every single person also present in the room. Quite why a Championship club would find it so difficult to sign players from Europe is another matter, but Riga and his agent maintain that their initial list of targets included both domestic and international players.

Blackpool had signed plenty of foreign-based players before, but for some reason problems arose with Riga's targets. Karl blamed intermediaries who were getting involved to 'broker' the deals. According to Karl, one deal for a player from Austria was agreed, until his agent called and said, 'We're about to get on the plane, I just need you to send me £150,000 to finalise the deal.' Thinking it was a joke, Karl laughed it off. 'No seriously,' the agent replied, 'otherwise he's not going.' In another deal with an Israeli club, Karl had allowed an intermediary to negotiate a transfer for two players who would arrive for a combined fee of £750,000. This was all being handled without his involvement, but he decided to call the club to see if he could get a better price. 'Right, we can't do that number. Just tell me honestly, what's the best price you can do?' The official on the other end replied, 'Look, I've already told your guys, it's £250,000.' Someone else was trying to get away with the extra £500,000.

It would be almost impossible to verify these stories and put names on paper, but it's not a retrospective work of fiction from Oyston. In an email to Riga dated 10 September 2014, Karl was expressing all these concerns to his manager. 'I have never experienced similar issues in my 16 years working in football,' Karl wrote. Oyston also told the BBC in an interview a week later, 'José wanted specific players.

They were from all over Europe and there were all sorts of mysteries attached … We can't make the same mistakes that other clubs have by putting money in Swiss bank accounts or sending players' wages to Greece so they can get it without paying tax.' Some Blackpool fans did note the irony that just a couple of years earlier, Karl had sanctioned placing £11m into his father's company for the explicit reason of reducing their own tax bill – the 'sound tax planning' which he was all too pleased to tell the media about at the time.

For his part, Riga denied having any first-hand knowledge of any problems, but admitted he struggled to take the allegations seriously, 'At the end I was for sure not convinced by what Karl Oyston was saying, of course not. I didn't see why I have to believe what Oyston said, I wanted to stay outside of this. I was just asking for players, not for money. I know that things like this can happen, but I was not looking for my bank account. I always consider that if you want to get rewards, it's through your work. And for me, being rewarded was being able to manage in England. I have never been in my career frustrated by the fact that another manager may earn more than me. I'm just looking for this short moment of pleasure when you get a good training session, when you get a win. That's it. Will the player be performing for Blackpool? That's it.'

Whatever was happening in negotiations, by far the biggest obstacle was simply attracting players to come to Blackpool and work in the conditions presented. Those who did arrive were set up in shabby hostels and B&Bs, with rooms in the club hotel often reserved for paying guests. Even if players did manage to get a room in the hotel, sometimes they would come back from an away trip to find their room had been given to a guest while they were away, their bags dumped at reception. Two players had to share a bunk bed in one hostel. Then they would go to training the next day and there was no food or water for them. There was already a culture shock for a foreign player arriving at Blackpool, or even a player coming up from London. Instead of being embraced and welcomed in, they were left to completely fend for themselves.

The situation came to a head on the first day of the new season. The opening day is always marked on the calendar for football fans everywhere, with dreams of what might lie ahead grasping the imagination of even the most cynical fan. At Blackpool, they were just hoping they'd be able to field a team. They were playing away at their old play-off foes Nottingham Forest. On the morning of the game, Riga was preparing his players at the hotel. He put a full team on the whiteboard, naming his starting XI and seven substitutes. 'Not great,' striker Steven Davies thought to himself, 'but we are where we are and that's what we've got. Fuck it, we'll see how we go.' Then, club secretary Chris Hough burst into the room and whispered into Riga's ear. 'Down … down,' Riga motioned to his assistant, who started taking names down off the board. What the fuck's going on?' one of the players asked.

Hough had to explain, 'Sorry, it's my fault, I forgot to register players in time.' Inexplicably, despite a late flurry of signings, they had started the day with only nine players confirmed to be registered. Instead of putting final preparations in place, Riga was worried they'd have to forfeit and take an automatic 3-0 defeat. Joan Oriol, signed from Spanish team Osasuna six days earlier, had not yet received international clearance. Neither had José Cubero, who was still awaiting confirmation of his work permit. The most recent transfers, Jeffrey Rentmeister and Joël Dielna, had signed after the midday Friday deadline to be eligible for the match. Somehow, Ishmael Miller, a domestic player who was signed three days before the game, was still not registered. Even worse, the club were worried Sergei Zenjov may not be eligible, with the forward only cleared to play moments before the team sheet was handed in at 2pm. His arrival had been announced over a month earlier. After some scrambling, Riga was able to put a new team up. A different starting line-up, and now with only four substitutes, two called up from the under-18s.

Nobody had a bad word to say about Chris Hough as a person, but he was brought in on the cheap and didn't seem wholly comfortable handling the operations at a Championship football club, especially one that had to rush through so many transfers in a short space of time. Matt Williams was described by many as doing the jobs of at least three people, and whoever took over had to be able to do the same. Hough had to find his feet in a hectic summer. His office was described as a bomb site, with papers scattered everywhere. Anybody who saw it wasn't surprised that he hadn't got the players registered in time.

On the bus on their way to Nottingham Forest's stadium, players were still trying to get registered, desperately hoping the authorities would take pity on them. There was only one senior outfield player on the bench, and just to make the numbers work midfielder David Perkins was slotted in to start at left-back. Unsurprisingly, they lost 2-0, but showed promise and fought hard in a game where a charitable observer may have said they deserved a point. They ultimately succumbed to a Forest team with the better quality on the day, and also in the battle against exhaustion.

Their lack of fitness work in pre-season, with delay after delay to the start of training, gave them little chance to compete for 90 minutes.

After the game, Riga told the press he wanted ten more signings in the transfer window. It was a remarkable position to be in, with the season already underway and a little over three weeks left until the deadline. He got half that, and the five players who did join were all free transfers, sitting around without a club until Blackpool made the call. Riga emailed Karl, 'If you are able to attract other players with more qualities for cheaper wages, okay. I just know that what was offered is not decent for this player. Why are you always discussing about wages even when the wages asked are more than acceptable?' Oyston left for a family holiday two weeks before deadline day, unable to be reached on the phone. It brought the operation of the club to a standstill. Nobody else at Bloomfield Road had the authority to sanction transfers. After 16 August, Blackpool didn't sign another player in the rest of the window. On the pitch, they were struggling to get off the ground and lost their first five games.

Riga faced more challenges. The promises Oyston made about improving the training ground failed to materialise. His assistant manager, Bart De Roover, departed in the first week of September, citing the lack of playing budget and terrible condition of the facilities. It had been a huge opportunity for him, he'd never coached in a league anywhere near as competitive and reputable. But it wasn't worth it. He decided he couldn't carry on working for Karl Oyston. For the few months he had, he went unpaid. Karl took to the *Gazette* to speak about the issue. 'He knew exactly what he was coming to when he came and if he didn't, more fool him. The fact he's reacted the way he has after not getting his own way probably says a lot about him.' Then, Oyston wisecracked that De Roover's natural level was the lower leagues in Belgium and that the club 'backed his decision to return'.

Instead of hiring a new number two, Blackpool were in the market for a new manager. Oyston blasted Riga's decision to fly home to Belgium during the first international break, with the team still seeking their first win. It was a contentious issue, although a senior player remarked that the team didn't see any particular controversy in it. Preparations were put in place in advance. The awful start to the season may have warranted extra sessions during the break, but there was also merit in taking a step back and recharging the batteries. When Riga returned to work, Oyston was scheming behind his back to find his replacement. He turned to former Burnley boss Owen Coyle, who had already rejected the Blackpool job twice before. His star had greatly dimmed in the years since leaving Turf Moor, but both sides suddenly looked a bit more desperate for the other to give them a kick-start. He was named as the bookies' favourite and the tabloids expected the deal to be announced imminently. Then, a couple of days later, the *Daily Mail* revealed talks had stalled. Chris Hough was actually on his way to Coyle's house with the paperwork, having reached a verbal agreement, but had to turn around at the last second as Coyle pulled out of the running. He was scared off with everything he was hearing out of the club. His agent, brother of ex-Pool player Mike Sheron, was also strongly steering him away from the job, having fallen out with Karl years previously.

Riga, still very much employed by Blackpool, wrote to Karl the following day, 'I read and hear a lot of things regarding the fact that you are looking for another manager. I guess that all this is untrue and I would like to have a meeting with you to speak about this situation. In my head, I am still your manager doing my best to prepare the team for the next game. Just let me know when we can meet, knowing that now I go for the training.' After the Coyle deal fell through, Oyston tried to bring in Gary Rowett from Burton Albion, but he rejected the opportunity. Burton released an official statement confirming the approach had been made. Before that point, the search had been the stuff of tabloid headlines. When Riga and his agent demanded answers from Karl, he batted it away as journalists making up rumours. Now, it was impossible to deny.

The move angered fans, who had hoped the Coyle story was false. Despite the results, the Blackpool faithful still supported Riga, who was becoming a martyr-like figure. His silence in the media gave people the opportunity to project their own narratives on to him, as they imagined the blazing rows he was having with Karl. They were all too happy to back the one not named Oyston. At one game, a fan delivered Riga a giant card on which he'd collected dozens of signatures showing support for the manager. People added messages like 'stick with it', 'don't give up', and 'we want you to stay'. He also had encouragement from elsewhere. Valeri Belokon got in touch from Latvia to let him know he was hoping to one day buy the club, and if he did, he would give him all the financial support he needed. He would often see Owen Oyston at the club restaurant, who didn't promise the same help, but did offer him an alternative career in modelling if it didn't work out, and invited him to his home for a photo shoot. Riga declined.

Blackpool finally got their first win in a televised night match at home to Cardiff, 11 games into the season. The occasion had been marked in advance as an opportunity to protest in front of the Sky cameras. In the 19th minute fans released black balloons and loud chants of 'we want Oyston out' echoed around Bloomfield Road. In the 53rd minute there was a mass walkout and the ground largely emptied. Those who left didn't see François Zoko's winning goal, but they didn't particularly care. The statement was more important and it had been delivered with great publicity. The win provided little momentum. After another international break, Blackpool were battered 4-2 by Huddersfield, managing to make the scoreline somewhat respectable after going down 3-0 within quarter of an hour. Riga started one of his summer signings, Joël Dielna, at left-back. It was only his third appearance of the season and his performance was so disastrous that he was hauled off after 16 minutes, right after the third goal went in. The summer transfer window had been littered with similar signings, who were simply out of their depth and couldn't handle the demands of Championship football. They brought in Nile Ranger, a once promising youngster who had been discarded by team after team due to an endless list of personal troubles. He was described as the most talented player in training, but couldn't keep out of his own way. He would constantly turn up late for training. At times he would drive in early to make sure he was on time, but would still end up missing the session after he fell asleep in his car while parked outside.

The senior members of the squad, who did have experience in the league, were disgusted with the attitude of some of the new arrivals. After defeats, they were joking around in the dressing room, boasting about a small piece of skill they had pulled off. It incensed one veteran, who tore into a group who were laughing among themselves, right after a match where they'd just lost to a last-minute penalty. Finally, 14 games in, bottom of the league and seven points off safety, Riga was sacked. Oyston had Chris Hough call to deliver the news for him. They had won one game.

The next managerial search didn't take long, Oyston had no doubt lined things up ahead of time. Lee Clark was named as Riga's replacement, although it would take a Herculean effort for him to turn the ship around. If there was any hope of survival it surely rested on the new manager bounce so many clubs seem to get when making a change mid-season. But Clark's first ten games made similarly grim reading, picking up just eight points, and Blackpool entered the new year further adrift at the bottom of the league. Clark managed to bring some real experience into the team, signing Jamie O'Hara, Nyron Nosworthy, Darren O'Dea and Chris Eagles on short-term deals. They added some quality, but age and a lack of fitness held them back. The names on the team sheet may have been more familiar to fans at the ground, but they still went into every game with an alarming talent deficit.

There remained a lack of professionalism in the team. In late December, a Snapchat was leaked from on-loan winger Jacob Murphy. It was a selfie of him smiling to the camera, with a caption that read 'we are going to lose … again' taken before a game. Murphy was sent packing back to his parent club Norwich City. Not only that, but Nile Ranger had gone AWOL. Clark sent out an appeal for help, 'If anyone can let us know where he is, send me a letter and we will go from there. I don't know where he is, I haven't seen him for more than two weeks. He's been asked to report into training and has been asked to play in games and he hasn't been seen.' He'd returned back to his home in London and didn't play again for the club.

Blackpool were supplying sportswriters with plenty of ink for their Christmas presents. The story broke that Karl Oyston had been engaging in vicious text exchanges with fans. Protests were becoming more vociferous and Karl's number had been shared on social media for a while. Despite the barrage of abuse he was getting at all hours of the day and night, he hadn't seemed interested in changing it. In fact, he was giving as good as he got. Fans would call Karl after a loss as he was driving back in his car and he would put them on loudspeaker, entertaining them as he made his journey home. He would put his phone on the middle of the desk in meetings for everyone else to hear. During one televised game a group of fans were sat in the pub and decided to call Karl at half-time. To their surprise, he answered and spent the next 15 minutes talking with them. The fans looked up to the TV screen and saw a Sky camera had zoomed in on Karl in the directors' box while he was on the phone. Even they thought the whole thing was completely surreal.

Then came Stephen Smith, whose texts with Karl were becoming more and more repugnant. Goaded on by friends, Smith tried to ensnare Oyston into saying the most heinous things he could, so he could leak it to the media. Karl fell for it hook, line and sinker. The result didn't look good for either side. It escalated first with Smith calling Karl a 'financial retard', but he was a fan nobody knew, the other was the chairman of a football club in charge of a multi-million-pound business. So, when Karl wrote back 'sorry your life's so shit but that's your fault not mine, enjoy the rest of your special needs day out', the newspapers destroyed him. The texts got worse. 'Are you sure we have met?' Karl asked, 'I would have remembered such a massive retard.' Then came, 'I do ask for help just not from an intellectual cripple like you. You are hilariously stupid as your type always are … get real you thick twat.' Oyston and Blackpool were once again the embarrassment of the football world, as the story was picked up by the BBC and all the national newspapers. It was a peek inside how Karl talked to those around him. The language he used in the texts was no different than the language he used on a daily basis to talk about anyone he didn't like.

To another fan, Karl cracked that his aim was to get the club to spiral all the way down to the non-league. He dubbed it 'Operation Conference' and said 'I am a never-ending nightmare revenge mission.' It prompted minority shareholder Valeri Belokon to give an interview to a local radio station, where he called for Karl to resign. For the first time in public, he suggested he was interested in buying the club, which gave a beacon of hope to all fans listening in. They were also hoping the EFL would hand down a suitable punishment on Oyston. There was a lot of rhetoric about how the language used was unacceptable and how they had zero tolerance for such matters. But in the end, he was banned from footballing activities for six weeks and given a £40,000 fine. Life continued on as normal inside Bloomfield Road.

Karl was spiralling out of control. Whenever he intervened to arrest the fall the club was in, he only created new problems. Throughout his tenure, one of his strengths, which many ex-staff members praised, was how he allowed his manager to get on with the job undisturbed. Even that changed in the 2014/15 season. Lee Clark had promoted youngsters Mark

Waddington and Dom Telford to the first team. They weren't going to save the team from relegation alone, but it was a lone bright spot to see two local lads breaking through. They grabbed their opportunities and impressed in their cameo appearances. The pair were still on youth contracts, so Karl offered them professional deals reportedly worth just £200 per week, with bonuses on top. Worse, with relegation looking close to a certainty, they'd be getting large pay cuts six months in. Blackpool had lost one of their brightest youth prospects in years, Harrison McGahey, the previous summer. After breaking into the first team at the end of the season, he'd left for lower-league Sheffield United, who offered better facilities and higher wages. Oyston was determined not to let that happen again. He ordered Clark to drop Waddington and Telford and forced them to leave first-team training and go back to the youth team.

Clark addressed the issue in the media, 'It's been a sad and tough few days for me personally. I think the world of them both as young lads and young footballers. Mark was outstanding at Aston Villa, and one of the most pleasurable moments I've had since coming here was seeing Dom's smile when he scored against Rotherham. I want them in my group … I've advised the chairman how important these players are to me and I want them around us. I can't do any more.' The situation lasted for a few weeks with no progress in sight, until Oyston finally backed down and allowed their return. Clark gave them both minutes in a game against Brighton at the end of January, in one of the season's rare victories. After the season finished, the pair departed for Stoke and more lucrative wages.

Oyston forced more changes to the team. By now, Blackpool were actually in something of an upturn in

Brett Ormerod mobbed by supporters on the Bloomfield Road pitch after securing a spot in the Championship play-offs in 2010.

Charlie Adam's iconic celebration after scoring his free kick at Wembley.

Ian Holloway walks off the Old Trafford pitch as Blackpool suffer relegation on the final day of the season.

Owen Oyston taking a seat before a game.

Karl Oyston with his son Sam.

Player-manager Barry Ferguson angrily throws back a tennis ball after a protest live on TV stopped play

Supporters make their way to the stadium together in protest on 'Judgement Day'

Supporters leave scarves and other memorabilia at the site of the Stan Mortensen statue, removed by the club.

Protesters in fancy dress as Owen and Karl Oyston, counting the 'Premier League millions'

Latvian club president Valeri Belokon arriving at the High Court during his case against the Oystons.

The 'BST Office' where fans picketed outside the ground each game, celebrating the appointment of the Court Appointed Receiver and removal of the Oystons. Chair Christine Seddon is fifth from the left and Tim Fielding is far right.

form. They'd only lost three of their last nine games, by far their best spell of the season. They were still bottom of the table, but were only six points off safety. They weren't cut adrift yet. In extremely difficult circumstances, Clark was squeezing results out of the players. Any other team would be doing everything in its power to fight for survival. So, fans were shocked at the unexpected news that goalkeeper Joe Lewis was to be dropped for the next game away at Watford. Lewis had joined in the summer in something of a coup for the beleaguered club. At one point he'd been touted as one of the best goalkeepers outside the Premier League, capped all the way up to England under-21 level. He hadn't lived up to those high expectations, but he was still arguably Blackpool's best player. If there was a list of reasons why the team was doing so badly, Lewis was near the very bottom. Yet for some reason, Clark decided to drop him in favour of Elliot Parish, who had never played a Championship game before. He'd only played 37 league games in his entire career, all at lower levels. It did not go well. Blackpool went into half-time with a 2-0 lead, before coming back out for the second half and collapsing. Watford got one back, equalised, and went ahead. Then they ran up the score, battered and humiliated their opponents, and scored some more until the Blackpool players looked at the referee and begged to be put out of their misery. The game ended and the scoreboard informed the crowd Watford had won 7-2, in case anyone had lost count. Afterwards, it was reported that Clark was told to drop Lewis because the club wanted to avoid triggering a clause in his contract. If he played 40 games that season, Blackpool would be forced to buy him permanently, paying £40,000 to his parent club Cardiff. He played 34 games.

Lewis made headlines later in the year after it was noticed during a game that he was wearing a shirt with his own autograph on it. He had signed his goalkeeper's top for the club to give away as a raffle prize to a sponsor. But when it came to matchday, they realised there was no spare one at hand. Someone had to rush to get the shirt back from the sponsor, who by now had it framed and hanging on his wall. They retrieved it just in time for the game, and the media reported the story with great glee. The club had been relegated to a punchline.

As the season drew to a close, the 'Not A Penny More' boycott continued to grow. The connection between the community and its football team had been ripped apart. The club was dying a slow death and thousands could only watch on solemnly. Local businesses suffered. Having been once booming with foot traffic from 16,000 fans coming weekly during the Premier League season, now they were catering to the scraps of what was left. Fans did what they could to help. Blackpool Supporters' Trust made a point of asking people to support the businesses around the stadium. These were the things the Oyston family never understood, nor cared to. Blackpool FC wasn't just 11 players on the pitch on a Saturday afternoon, it was a communal institution. The town's fortunes could be lifted or fall in unison with the success of the team. It was a point of pride when their club rose to take on the Premier League giants, but now it had been left to rot. A generation of children were missing out on growing up with heroes in tangerine to support. Parents were missing out on valuable family time with them. Weekly pilgrimages to Bloomfield Road were part of the bond family members had, not just on the Fylde coast, but all around the country. There was an absence, a hole. It was like having a family member on life support. In an act of sacrilege, some Blackpool fans even wanted their team to lose. There was no Blackpool FC any more, it was Oyston FC. Oyston FC had to lose every week. They had to be starved of any oxygen and resources. No more money, no more support. Only after Oyston FC died could Blackpool FC return.

The last game of the season came at home to Huddersfield. Blackpool had long since been relegated in spectacular fashion, sitting on 25 points with 45 games gone and assured of the indignity of having the lowest points total in the division's history. It was only fitting that such an awful season would be given a formal honour. They hadn't won a single game in 17, losing 12. It had been a prolonged period of abject failure, stretching way back into the previous season. Over the last 517 days, Blackpool had played 78 competitive fixtures. They won seven, drew 20, and lost 51.

BST and the Tangerine Knights were working together to organise the biggest demonstration yet for the final game. Many fans had been staying away from Bloomfield Road but still had season tickets, hooked in early by false promises and the cheap ticket deal. There was a collective resignation that the game would be their last. The battle lines had been drawn. Those going to protest were ready for whatever consequences came their way. It was named 'Judgement Day', after an infamous interview Karl Oyston gave at the start of the season where he defended the club's disastrous summer, and asked people to 'judge me at the end of the season'.

In anticipation of the demonstration, Karl ordered the removal of a statue of club legend and ex-England striker

Stan Mortensen. Mortensen had scored nearly 200 goals for Blackpool, including a hat-trick at Wembley to win the 1953 FA Cup. His was the first statue erected outside the redeveloped Bloomfield Road. Oyston claimed he feared it would be damaged in the protest. Earlier in the week someone had put through some windows at the stadium by hurling rocks, but it was a flimsy excuse. The removal was an attempted bastardisation of what the day was going to be. It was an effort to frame protesters as little more than thugs, thoughtlessly destroying anything in their path. Fans held a march along the promenade and around the stadium before kick-off. It was held peacefully. They laid wreaths and scarves at the base of Morty's statue, which had visible damage from the hack job done to remove it – not by fans, but by the club itself. Among the organisers of the protest, they couldn't help but crack a smile when the statue was taken down. It was an unforced error by Oyston, rightly seen through by all as yet another attempt at antagonising the fanbase. When pictures surfaced of the damage the removal had done, it only encouraged more to join in with the demonstrators. It was the literal manifestation of how the Oystons were destroying the legacy of the club.

Thousands joined the march and walked together, unfurling banners, scarves, and a whole variety of makeshift signs with anti-Oyston remarks. Despite marking a solemn end to the season, it was a party-like atmosphere. Fans chanted and jeered; they came together in a way they hadn't been able to in years. People from all walks of life, for one moment, joined together in a common interest. There was a smaller group who were going to rush on to the pitch during the game. They expected banning orders but they didn't care. The plan was to do it at the start of the second half. By coming out of the concourse as normal after the break, it would catch stewards off guard. When the moment came, a flood of supporters ran on the pitch and the players were quickly escorted off. One or two stewards enthusiastically caught fans and dragged them down to the ground, but the rest let the mass of people rush on, quickly culminating in around 200 people gathering in the centre circle. Chants of 'We want Oyston out!' and 'Oyston is a wanker!' engulfed the stadium. Even the Huddersfield fans sang along. Someone let off a smoke bomb and the tangerine clouds lifted high into the fading blue sky, supplying the backdrop for a line of fans facing the directors' box, looking straight at Karl Oyston. The TV cameras showed him sat with his son Sam, a bemused and arrogant smile across his face. 'Shall we take a selfie?' he asked.

A wall of stewards separated them, but there was no effort to remove the fans once they got there. The police knew in advance of the planned protest and recognised the spirit in which it was being done. One of the police officers who had liaised with the Tangerine Knights was a Newcastle fan. He was well aware of how important a football club could be to its community, and the problems that could arise with ownership. He'd even been on the pitch himself at St James' Park to protest against Mike Ashley. The Blackpool fans sat down in the centre circle. They were going to force the cancellation of the game and wouldn't move for anything less. It was something British football had never seen before. A lull was interrupted by the sight of a man in a motorised wheelchair driving on to the pitch to join the crowd, to roaring laughter and applause. More flares erupted. Fans sang and beckoned others on to join them. After an hour, it was finally announced that the game had been called off. It was a small victory, but one they had earned. It was headline news and drew attention to their plight. This was no ordinary match. This was no ordinary club. The game was awarded a 0-0 result and, amazingly, the fans had performed better on the pitch that season than the players. At a point a game, they would have ended with 46 points, much higher than the 26 the team finished on.

As things died down, a handful of people managed to get their way past security and climb up the stand to the directors' box where Karl Oyston and his family stood inside. Five fans were arrested, including Mark Rushton, who managed to get right up to the glass doors. Wearing a Guy Fawkes mask, he started pounding away with clenched fists, trying to pull it open, before being dragged away by the police. In court, Karl's wife Victoria gave emotional testimony about how terrified she was for her safety and for her children. A police sergeant at the scene described how nervous he was at what might happen. His nerves were not entirely directed at the actions of Rushton, however. He alleged that he'd seen Karl goading fans up to the directors' box, waving them forward with his hands, and ignored repeated calls to stop. Karl denied this claim. Rushton received a jail sentence for his crime. Meanwhile, the question over whether Karl incited it was left ignored by the court.

In the grand scheme of things, the Huddersfield protest may have amounted to little more than a collective blowing-off of steam. A cathartic release of anger. But those moments were important. The fans would convene together at the end of every season for 'Judgement Day 2' and 'Judgement Day 3', but the picket line was never to be crossed again. Dozens were hit with legal letters from the club for encroaching on the pitch, with threats of penalties up to £50,000. One recipient was Pauline O'Rourke, a lifelong fan who'd been a club volunteer for years, organising travel to games for a supporters' group for young children. Her husband, Billy, had played for Blackpool in the 80s. She hadn't been on the pitch, but her twin sister had. Knowing her face, the Oystons sent her threatening letters, alleging criminal activity. She was devastated. She feared for what might happen to her, and the betrayal from the club she had poured so much unpaid time into helping turned a huge part of her world upside down. After she told them of their mistake the letters stopped, but they never apologised.

The others took their bans and moved on. They had no intention of returning any time soon. The next phase of the protests was for a long, slow, boring squeeze on the finances. Each relegation meant less money in competition bonuses and TV revenue, leaving the club relying mostly on income from match tickets and concession sales. The hope for the NAPM boycott was that if the fans stopped going, the club would become loss-making. At that point, there would be nothing left for the Oystons to stick around for. It would be a gradual, drawn-out process. Fans were preparing themselves for years in the wilderness. But they had a glimmer of hope that a quicker resolution could be found. Across the North and Baltic Seas and into Latvia, Valeri Belokon was ready to take the Oystons on in court.

Chapter 7

War and Peace

AS BLACKPOOL were preparing for their new life in League One, reports surfaced that an old legend might be returning. Lee Clark had departed following relegation, and Ian Holloway was tipped for the vacant job. His journey hadn't fared much better than Blackpool's after he left in 2013. Despite winning promotion with Crystal Palace, he was sacked early on in the Premier League campaign. He moved on to Millwall but was axed before completing a full season, with the club languishing in the relegation zone. Whatever magic he'd sprinkled on the Blackpool team had failed to produce the same success in future stops. Improbably, a return made sense. But there was hesitancy on all sides. In other circumstances, the return of the manager who'd achieved so much and brought so much joy would be a welcome boost, but by now, Blackpool had been splintered, torn apart with no prospect of being repaired. There was no run of form, no promotion or great season that could bring back those who had drawn their line in the sand, never to return with the Oystons at the helm. They rooted for the club's demise. For loss after loss, Saturday after Saturday. Every win was a vindication of what the Oystons were doing, every loss inched them closer to the exit. Fans who did attend faced derogatory abuse. They were mocked as 'scabs' for putting their own short-term satisfaction above the fight to secure a long-term future for the club. New managers were disregarded from the day they walked in as simple lackeys, pawns for the Oystons.

It was a no-win scenario. When Holloway's interest became public, the Tangerine Knights released an open letter, writing, 'Ian, we respectfully urge you to reconsider. This club is in turmoil, and it is our opinion that Karl has lost control of the club. You must have seen what has happened and that there is a civil war here between the fans and the Oystons. That is not going to end by you returning here, it will only paper over the cracks. No matter what happens, until that family leaves Blackpool this club is going nowhere. Please Ian, don't come back whilst the Oyston family are still in control of our club.'

Blackpool FC was the club Ian Holloway had fallen in love with. It was a club and a town that shared his own oddities and eccentricities, and allowed him to express everything he wanted to try on the football pitch. It gave him complete freedom to play football the way he felt it ought to be played. That club no longer existed.

Holloway had his own fears. He didn't know if he could work with Karl again. He made an agreement that he would only return if ex-club secretary Matt Williams came back too. The two had enjoyed a productive and fruitful relationship, keeping each other sane and finding ways to work around Karl. Williams decided he would also only re-join if Holloway came back. The two tied their fortunes together. They made their interest known and awaited the call from the club. 'Have you heard anything?' one rang the other. 'No, have you?' They got their answer watching Sky Sports News. After a few days of silence, it flashed with the breaking news that Karl had hired Neil McDonald to be the new manager.

Whatever the future may have held if the duo had come back, it could hardly have gone much worse than the 2015/16 season eventually did. In some respects, the job should have been easier for manager and chairman alike. With fans staying away, there was less scrutiny, less interruption. There was no fear of a game being suspended due to protest. However, if such benefits did exist, they didn't show on the pitch. For all the concern about what effect fan demonstrations had on the team, they fared worse when playing to a pacified, mostly empty stadium. The blanket of failure from the previous years proved impossible to shake off.

McDonald came in with expectations, like any new manager would. He believed he could be the person to give the club a fresh start. In pre-season, putting on a brave face in front of the cameras, he seemed to suggest wins on the pitch would have fans coming back in their droves. It was a poor misunderstanding of what was wrong with the club, and their resilience to change it. During McDonald's introductory press conference, a reporter for the *Blackpool Gazette* was denied entry by Karl Oyston in his latest attempt to clench a tighter control over the narrative. He had thrown the *Gazette* out once before in the late 90s, banning them from the ground and refusing them access to the fixture list for the upcoming season. His reasoning was that they 'took from the club and provided nothing', and he changed tact only once they started paying for sponsorship. Forget the column inches, forget having the front and back pages of the town's largest publication all devoted to the football club, all that free publicity and promotion. If they weren't directly putting money into BFC's bank account, why let them in? It was less clear what prompted the latest ban, the club gave no reason to the newspaper. It didn't take much deduction to figure out, however, that the *Gazette* had likely stirred the wrath of Karl Oyston after they dropped his weekly column as a reaction to 'textgate' a few months before.

Pre-season started with yet more controversy. The state of the Bloomfield Road pitch had been a disaster across the previous two years and was universally condemned for being unsafe to play on. On Twitter, fans questioned why the club was hosting a Neil Diamond concert at the ground that summer, fearing it would cut up the turf even more. After the gig, pictures surfaced showing visible damage. There were three weeks left before the start of the season. An account called @CommercialBFC, which had previously been advertised by the main BFC page as being one of their affiliates, decided to participate in the discussion. It had been a civil one until the commercial account replied 'typical arsehole wankers!!!' at the fans bemoaning the decision. When others responded with incredulity, it tweeted, 'So nobody is allowed to answer back when they get a load of grief? We've just got to take it?' Once again, the sports news desks were lighting up with the latest drama at Bloomfield Road. The club was forced to release a statement claiming the account was no longer affiliated with them. It is believed that a former employee ran it, someone close to Karl, but he was no longer on their payroll.

There was also the curious case of Nile Ranger, who hadn't played since November, but had been informed the club were taking up the one-year option on his contract to extend his stay. He was already facing weekly fines on his £7,800 yearly contract, and he hadn't been seen for months. New manager Neil McDonald told him he wouldn't be allowed anywhere near his first team, and when he did arrive for pre-season training (four weeks late), he was kept away from the ground and left to run up and down sand dunes in an effort to get fit. There was no reason for Oyston to pick up his deal, few other teams would even offer him a trial, they certainly wouldn't pay Blackpool a fee for him. Ranger alleged Oyston made the decision purely out of spite, to stop him being able to join another club for free.

The season started with less fanfare. Not many people around the town could name more than a handful of players. Wins and losses passed with little consideration or care, although there were more of the latter than the former. The last game of the season was in early May, where Blackpool needed three points and favourable results elsewhere to avoid consecutive relegations. They were hammered 5-1 by a mediocre, mid-table Peterborough team. Five years had passed since they were playing at Old Trafford, fighting to stay in the Premier League. Three relegations and eight managers later, through protests and boycotts, court cases and endless fighting, Blackpool had fallen to the bottom of English football.

At the end of the season, the recently retired Brett Ormerod was offered a testimonial match as a recognition and celebration of his career. It spanned many different clubs, but none as close to his heart as Blackpool. He rejected the opportunity to play the game at Bloomfield Road, and reflected mournfully on the situation, 'There isn't anybody in this country at the moment who doesn't understand that Blackpool is a club at war with itself. I can't see how it's going to be resolved really. If the Oystons sold up and left, the fans would flock back. Everything about Blackpool is negative.' Ormerod requested that funds from the day go towards the Gary Parkinson Trust to help his ongoing financial concerns, adding his voice to other ex-pros criticising the lack of support from the club. 'I'm not sure Blackpool really did anything. You'd have to ask them why. If we can do something for him, I know I'll be able to sleep at night.'

The game was held at neighbouring non-league team AFC Fylde and 3,600 Blackpool fans watched, united together inside a football stadium for the first time in years. The nostalgia ran through different eras of special Blackpool teams Ormerod had been a part of. He played alongside his old strike partner John Murphy, being fed passes from the likes of David Vaughan and Keith Southern from the 2010 Premier League side. They played in a specially designed tangerine kit created by fan Lee Morton. Morton released a line of unofficial merchandise to allow supporters to proudly represent their team and their own boycotting efforts, without money going to the Oystons. Fans clapped and cheered as old favourites ran out in a still-familiar tangerine. It was a celebration of the past, but also a glimpse into what the future could yet hold. The ritual of going to the football, walking through crowded streets around the stadium and feeling a warm buzz in the air. Buying a pre-match pie and pint. Standing next to a total stranger and striking up a conversation about preferred tactical manoeuvres. Winning, losing, but above all just being there. That was what they were reminded of, what they had to keep fighting for.

That Blackpool were able to make an immediate return to League One under new manager Gary Bowyer was of little interest to most fans. Only 5,000 made the trip to Wembley, where they defeated Exeter in the play-off final. There were suspicions the true number was even smaller than the one announced, and those who were there looked drowned in a sea of empty seats in the 90,000-capacity stadium. The rest watched on back home and smiled in satisfaction. It was a painful sacrifice. Even without the same connection they once had, days at Wembley for play-off finals are those special occasions that should be memorialised forever. Many would have happily dropped to the depths of non-league football if it meant getting rid of the Oystons, but few were so cynical they couldn't at least enjoy the result on the day, even if they weren't there to celebrate it.

With promotion secured, there was no looking ahead to the future. There was no sudden clamour to scroll through the live blogs and search social media to unearth rumours about new signings. Thousands of fans did not congregate to purchase season tickets for the upcoming campaign. By now, the real entertainment was the court case about to play out between both owners of the club. It would dictate the very future of Blackpool FC. It would decide whether fans had any prospect of walking back through the turnstiles at Bloomfield Road.

Valeri Belokon had instructed his lawyers to begin a legal case against the Oystons over two years previously. They spent their time diligently building a case for unfair prejudice. Their claim alleged that Belokon had been frozen out of decision-making and was not paid his fair share of the money Owen Oyston had taken out. They scored an early win in a smaller case, over the development of the new South Stand. Belokon had loaned the club £4.75m to aid construction, Owen pitched in £1m. Belokon was due 50 per cent of the income from the stand in order to repay the loan with interest, but only £180,000 had been returned by November 2011. After that, the Oystons turned the tap off, using losses from other construction outside of their agreement to justify non-payment. The judge ruled in Belokon's favour, netting him a small seven-figure sum. It was 1-0, although in reality the case paled in comparison to the main event in June 2017.

What everyone was waiting for was the pivotal judgment in the hands of Justice Marcus Smith, who was overseeing the proceedings. For Blackpool fans, there weren't any other catalysts on the horizon. There was no mystery investor publicly expressing his desire to buy the club. Owen Oyston seemed more determined than ever to carry on, and it was later revealed he had ignored an offer from a consortium that eventually went on to buy Bradford. The boycotts were having a great effect on the money coming in, but the office space rentals in the stadium guaranteed a certain level of income. As did whatever sponsorship deals they managed to cobble together and the centrally distributed broadcasting payouts. It might not have been the final roll of the dice, but it was their best one.

Belokon was being represented by Clifford Chance, commonly ranked among the top five law firms in the world. Andrew Green and Fraser Campbell were the barristers instructed to deliver the result. They were in complete control from the very start. They revealed the astuteness of their tactics by pushing for the smaller South Stand case first, despite naturally impatient Blackpool fans wishing they would go for the jugular. They hired stenographers, unusual for such a case, to transcribe every word the witnesses said. They locked the Oystons into testimony, crucial evidence they relied on in the main proceedings. It finally started in June.

Green and Campbell were leading a case unlike any other they had ever worked on. No other had such a captive audience. No other had such a direct impact on an entire community. Blackpool supporters travelled down to London, some dressed in their tangerine football shirts, watching and showing their support as if they were back on the Bloomfield Road terraces. There was an appointed transcriber each day, reporting back with verbatim transcripts. In their thousands, fans peeped at their phones under office desks. They switched between spreadsheets and online tabs, avoiding the watchful eye of the boss. They clung to whatever scrap of info they could get, any inkling from a line of questioning or hint from body language.

Clifford Chance were having fun. Alongside Green and Campbell were a group of young trainees watching on. All had laptops with A View From The Tower, the main fans' forum, open. They read along as fans dissected and commented on the day's play. Owen Oyston's team had come together late, after he decided to change his representatives. He had previously instructed the highly reputable firm Seddons, but they ended up falling out and the firm sued Owen for alleged lack of payments. It caused a major rupture in the family. Karl was pleading with him to listen to a settled team of legal experts, leading to regular screaming matches. The defence was weakened by a lack of unity. In court, father and son sat apart from each other. They rarely spoke. Those around him described Owen as restless, unable to sit back and follow the advice of the professionals. Alan Steinfeld was the man settled on to represent the defence, alongside barrister Eric Shannon, who had worked on the libel cases against fans. It was a cheaper team than what Seddons would have been, and a source familiar with the situation said Owen Oyston was determined to write as much of the defence as he could, although ultimately all documents submitted to the court would have had to have been settled on by the lawyers.

One of the main issues in the proceedings was whether or not Valeri Belokon was entitled to 50 per cent shareholding in the club. On paper he'd always been listed as the 20 per cent minority owner, but Clifford Chance were able to show that the initial idea had been for a joint venture. Internal emails between Owen's advisors, composed early on in the negotiation stage, referred to '50/50 parity'. A handwritten note mentioned the price of £4.5m. It also mentioned an issue of tax losses. Blackpool FC had accumulated losses of over £10m in previous years, which they could carry over and use to reduce a tax bill on later profits. If Oyston sold 50 per cent of the club for £4.5m, it's likely they would have lost most of that amount the moment the club turned a large enough profit, thanks to HMRC. Oyston got his team together to figure out a solution. They realised they could transfer the losses to another business in the Oyston empire as long as he continued to own at least 75 per cent of the club. Therein lay the problem: there was a cap on how much Belokon could own. Debate commenced as to how they could skirt the rules. They considered giving Belokon 20 per cent with a future option to raise it to 50, but the law didn't allow for such a loophole. Then they presented a draft agreement with another clever idea. Belokon would purchase 20 per cent, but through a separate company would provide a consultancy service. His fee would be exactly half of Blackpool FC's profits. Again, it was nixed. Owen continued to search for ways to achieve joint ownership, but with no clear answer, progress stalled.

It was Belokon who decided to push things along to find a conclusion, and all written agreement to 50 per cent was dropped. In June 2006, he paid £1.8m for a 20 per cent stake in the club. He followed up with two loans amounting to a further £2.7m, bringing his total investment to £4.5m. It did not pass by Justice Marcus Smith that the £2.7m, while not formalised as paying for the 'top up' 30 per cent of shares, did more than coincidentally match perfectly what was written as the price for 50 per cent. Clifford Chance presented evidence that an under-the-table 'gentleman's agreement' existed, whereby Belokon was equal shareholder, even if not on paper. That both sides effectively admitted to devising the plan to avoid a tax bill was more or less left notwithstanding. Karl Oyston had given an interview to the *Blackpool Gazette* a month after the agreement was signed, describing it as 'an initial 20 per cent investment with an option to take 50'. This was quite a blow to their defence. It was hard to argue that the agreement never existed when the chairman of the football club told the media it did at the time.

The judge found in favour of Belokon. The loans he provided after the purchase of shares – provided interest-free and unsecured, with scant prospect of return – made no commercial sense without such an agreement underwriting them. Part of the additional payment wasn't even a loan. A sum of £850,000 was given as a 'gift' for the purpose of buying players, with no requirement for repayment. The judge didn't accept testimony from one of Owen's witnesses that he had 'given Belokon a beating' in negotiations. The conclusion that Valeri and Owen were joint partners from day one informed much of Justice Smith's findings in the rest of the case.

In witness testimony, the Oystons produced a procession of their legal and financial advisors. Each stuck zealously to the script. Andrew Green set about picking them apart. Their answers were robotic and rehearsed, and the judge was not impressed. He described Owen's old solicitor, Anthony Dempsey, as overly protective, when he refused to imagine a scenario where a hypothetical deal could have existed without his knowledge. 'He had an impressive command of the documents and a singular knack of reconstructing what he thought must have happened,' Smith commented in his summation, 'But he had a significant, and I am sure unconscious, bias towards the interests of the Oyston side. Thus, when giving his understanding of some of the draft contractual documents, Mr Dempsey was dogmatic in suggesting a meaning that would not be the interpretation of the reasonable bystander.' Ian Cherry, the supposedly independent auditor of the club's financial accounts, came next. He was equally condemned, albeit in as polite and professional a way as possible, 'Mr Cherry acted as an advisor to the Oyston side in respect of transactions materially affecting Blackpool FC. No auditor, properly having regard to his responsibilities, should have placed himself in this position.' Smith went further to describe him as 'in the pocket' of the Oystons. Little weight was given to his analysis.

Blackpool fans delighted in the grilling Green gave in cross-examination. One by one he dissected Owen's men as they squirmed their way through questioning. Owen and Karl were to be the main event, but watching their foot soldiers be held to account brought nearly as much joy. Eventually, they got their moment to watch Karl step up to the witness box. The court could have charged for popcorn. Karl's strategy was to claim memory loss. Those at the back of the room had a running joke by keeping tally of the amount of times he would respond 'I don't recall' to a line of questioning. When pressed by Green, the nature of his dictatorial and bullying regime revealed itself. In summation, the judge held little back, 'He was an argumentative witness, who gave speeches rather than answering questions. I found him generally incapable of answering a question straightforwardly. He had a marked tendency, not to give evidence, but to advocate. This was not aided by the fact that his actual recollection of events was extremely poor … he was an unimpressive witness, and I cannot place very much weight on his evidence. As a person, Mr Karl Oyston seemed to me to be a forceful character, capable of firm and probably harsh leadership. When crossed, he could react badly and be quite rude.'

Andrew Green attacked from the start. In his witness statement, Karl had accused Belokon of inciting the fans and leaking confidential information. When pressed if such an accusation was fair, Karl repeatedly referred to the allegations and conviction Belokon had for money laundering activities. 'I never mentioned money laundering and you've already mentioned it three times in the first three minutes! Is your position anything goes?' Green barked, 'Is it true you don't take kindly to people that are against you? You are a bully!' Later, he asked Karl about the 'textgate' scandal, where he'd been caught name-calling fans using derogatory slurs. 'I made an apology, even though it was shameful provocation,'

Karl said. 'Even now you can't resist a dig, can you!' Green returned.

Then came Owen, who put on the best performance of all. He battled to what one observer described as a 'losing draw' on the first day, keeping up with questions and holding firm in his defence. It went about as well as he could realistically have hoped. Even the fans at the back, with little knowledge of the law or court proceedings, were mightily impressed by Green. An award-winning barrister, he had a masterful control over cross-examination. Rather than drilling down on one subject over and over again, raising in pitch and intensity as one might see in a TV show or film, he would swerve from subject to subject, weaving intricate threads and returning to them in crescendo. It would have exhausted even the most honest and well-disciplined witness. As he left court at the end of the day, Owen posed for a photo with a member of his legal team, holding a scarf with the words 'Oyston Out' written on it. He was not so pleased with the next day's outing.

On day two, the 82-year-old Owen looked every bit of his age. He was worn down by Green's zig-zagging questioning. He complained of difficulty hearing. He moaned that he had a 'head cold'. 'I'm having trouble finding my bundle of papers here because I'm an old man,' he offered. At one stage, he had his daughter come up to the box and sit next to him to turn the pages. Later, he went up to Marcus Smith's bench to sit next to him so he could hear him better. Smith indulged him, but nobody was really convinced. He was straight to attention as soon as an easier question was tossed his way. At one moment he was able to rattle off the exact number of board meetings that had occurred over several years. Green jumped on it, 'Come come now Mr Oyston, you are a wily old fox, aren't you! You can't remember this, but you know *exactly* how many meetings have taken place!' If it weren't for the demand for silence from the audience, oohs and aahs would have rung through the chamber.

Owen was stuttering through answers. He contradicted himself frequently. He forgot facts and details that a day earlier he had command over. Green picked apart discrepancy between his own testimony and his son's. 'Well, Karl must have misremembered,' Owen had to admit. Green switched through the gears. He rarely jumped in for the kill but pushed from second, to third, to fourth in real time. He had an uncanny recall ability, at all times able to spot an inconsistency within the thousands of transcribed words of testimony and hour upon hour of cross-examination. 'Well that's not what your financial controller said,' or 'that's not what Karl said,' were frequent interjections. In a standout 'gotcha' moment, Owen was discussing a decision made between himself and Karl, without the involvement of Valeri Belokon or his director Normunds Malnacs. This was a key part of Clifford Chance's case. They needed to prove the Oystons were freezing their client out of decision-making, and Owen was revealing a crucial piece of evidence. Andrew Green recognised this better than anyone. 'Can't you see that the decisions you were taking were prejudicial to Valeri's interests and he should have been involved?' he asked. Owen argued that subsequently, they had changed the way they operated to be more inclusive. 'Well that's going to be scant consolation to my client,' Green spat. 'Prejudice has already been suffered. It's too late for you to be making vague promises about changing your ways now.' The Blackpool fans licked their lips at every twist and turn. They were besotted.

Local artist Rob Purdon, who had catalogued the ongoing protests with irreverent cartoon drawings, created a special piece for the occasion. It showed Green and colleague Fraser Campbell grabbing a hapless Karl Oyston in a headlock. Another Blackpool fan who was at the trial, Scott Koudellas, had a copy. He noticed a boy and a girl sat next to the Clifford Chance lawyers. Thinking they were trainees, he showed them the cartoon. 'Oh my God, that's Dad!' one of them exclaimed. 'Send us that, Dad's famous!' At each day's conclusion, the lawyers for Clifford Chance would take time to talk to the fans at the back. They didn't reveal much in their conversations, but their body language and overall demeanour expressed a great confidence in their performance so far.

Once Justice Smith concluded that Belokon was in fact a 50/50 partner, what came next was the complicated process of figuring out how much money the Oystons had taken from the club. He looked at a series of transactions which he called 'disguised dividends'. Owen had never declared a formal dividend for himself, which would have also triggered payments to minority shareholders. That included not just Valeri Belokon, but a large group of individuals who had bought shares in the 70s and 80s, when Blackpool were trying to raise cash. They owned around four per cent of the club. Neither did Owen take a large salary, because he didn't want to pay the tax on it. Instead, he found other ways to profit. Following the money as it flowed out had been almost impossible for the sleuths connecting the dots at home. It proved difficult to entangle even for forensic accountants who took a stab at it. Transactions were often undocumented and signatures weren't required. Fans recoiled as the judge peeled back the curtain, exposing how the Oystons stripped the club of its money. They knew it would never come back, but it gave an element of closure. They had their day in court.

Owen had been at Blackpool since 1987. For the first decade and a half he pumped a good amount of money into the club, of this there is generally little dispute. However, the murkiness of the financial accounts and his propensity to embellish made it difficult to calculate the exact figure. His partnership with Belokon provided a helpful cut-off date. Their contractual agreement declared that the club was no longer liable for any debt owed to Owen, bar one modest loan of £210,000. So, when Owen gave his soliloquy to the court about how he saved the club and bankrolled it for years, it was essentially irrelevant. He had wiped those debts clean to create a more attractive landscape for outside investment. When Belokon joined, he was entering into a partnership intended to be built on a blank slate.

For three years their relationship commenced without visible friction, but it didn't always run smoothly. At a meeting early in the 2006/07 season, the board discussed the poor start the team was having and whether Simon Grayson should continue as manager. Karl Oyston recalled that while the rest of the board voted to sack Grayson, he refused. He claims he made an ultimatum, 'I'm the chairman. If you sack him, I'm walking too.' Gavin Steele, another director at the club, refuted this version of events, as did Normunds Malnacs, who was with Valeri for the meeting. He claimed that while Karl was steadfast in his backing of Grayson, neither he nor Belokon made any sort of declaration they wanted to sack him. They felt it was an informal, open discussion and were unhappy with Karl's revisionism. Malnacs said, 'He used this occasion to strengthen his tie with Simon – as if he was the good director defending Simon from evil foreigners who want to sack a good manager. Our inquiries were overblown into insisting on firing Simon, which was absolutely not true. This was the first of many episodes where the Oystons were playing games against us.'

Under Grayson, Blackpool's form improved drastically and they won promotion to the Championship at the end of the season. In December 2009, now with Ian Holloway in charge, they were flying high enough that reaching the Premier League became more than a far-off dream. Before Christmas, Owen Oyston emailed Valeri to inform him of an old debt that had resurfaced. In 2000, his other company, Zabaxe, had loaned Blackpool £944,652. That debt had been repaid by BFC's parent company, Segesta, in the form of shares. Segesta was owned by Owen and he used it as a holding company for the football club, a common business tactic to ring-fence associated assets. The email read, 'As a result of a legal technicality, that has now come to light, the share issue to Zabaxe was invalid.' The shares were reversed, and Blackpool FC was liable for the £944,652 again. Oyston assured Valeri that Segesta would take over the debt and make the repayment. It had to, because the 2006 partnership stipulated no money from Blackpool FC could be used to repay other loans. It was a confusing set of circumstances. Justice Smith commented, 'There is an air of unreality about all this formality.' But this is how the whole network operated. A decade-old liability resurfacing out of nowhere, involving three different companies all owned by one man, was par for the course.

In March 2010, the BFC board passed a special resolution that the Zabaxe debt would be taken off its hands and paid by Segesta. There seemed to be little discussion or disagreement of note, and it had been handled as expected. Everything changed two months later when Blackpool won the Championship play-off final at Wembley, and faced the prospect of nearly £100m coming into the club. The day after the game, Owen and Valeri met to talk about the team's incredible achievement. Owen proposed large bonuses for each shareholder, writing in his notes, 'I would like a minimum of £5m and maybe a couple of million more.' Over the next week, Owen got his team together to identify all the different liabilities they could find. Regardless of whatever agreement he had entered into, he wasn't about to let the opportunity pass by. Their first act was reversing the resolution they had passed two months earlier. The Zabaxe debt was now going to be paid by Blackpool FC after all. But that was just the tip of the iceberg.

Next came a figure of £4.2m owed by Segesta to a construction company called Protoplan. Protoplan was owned, typically, by Owen Oyston. It was incorporated and awarded a contract to build the new North and West stands when Bloomfield Road was being redeveloped at the start of the century. Protoplan didn't do much itself, it didn't have employees, but it hired contractors to complete the work. In 2005 this debt stood at £5.5m. Segesta was paying it off with income derived from the new stands. Importantly, this was an agreement between two other Oyston-owned companies, with nothing to do with Blackpool Football Club. The club itself didn't own the football stadium, Segesta did. Segesta was making payments to Protoplan year by year, leaving around £4.2m left in 2010. Owen asked his team to figure out a way to get money out of BFC to pay off the rest of the debt. The two Latvian directors on the board were purposefully left out of the discussions. Owen's accountant emailed him three days after the Wembley victory, warning him, 'The problem is that any income from football will go into Blackpool FC and it is my understanding that you agreed not to take this money out when you agreed the loan arrangement with Valeri Belokon.' Another advisor wrote, 'How can this be done? Do you have any ideas?' They all knew that using Blackpool's money broke the contract, but that didn't stop Owen.

In June, Owen held a meeting with his entire team, stating the objective plainly from the outset, 'Need to get funds without going through Belokon and without tax.' One note written by his solicitor read, 'Send the agreements to barrister as he wants to break it.' Evidence like this, laid out in black and white in the documents, was gold dust for Clifford Chance. In August 2010, by now getting wind that something was stirring, Normunds Malnacs emailed financial controller Rod Dyer to confirm the complete breakdown of all the liabilities both BFC and Segesta had. Dyer confirmed that nothing had changed since the 2006 agreement, and that the only debt BFC had was the £210,000 loan to Owen Oyston. Both the £944,652 Zabaxe debt and the £4.2m Protoplan debt were explicitly stated as Segesta's to discharge. Yet, three weeks later, Owen withdrew £4.2m from the Blackpool FC bank account and transferred it to Protoplan. That one transaction alone was more than the club spent on transfer fees the entire year in the Premier League. After another few months, Owen took the £944,652 from the club too.

The Latvians discovered the bank transfer and Malnacs responded immediately, 'This transaction seems to be out of scope of the concluded agreements between the two major shareholders. Therefore, I would like to draw your attention to a need for a board meeting to resolve the issue.' This moment changed everything in the so far relatively easy relationship between the two sides. It triggered discussions on how to move forward, escalating to a suggestion that Belokon sell his shares and exit. The relationship fractured. Valeri had invested nearly £11m in the club since joining. Owen had put in just £1m. While Valeri was pushing for the return on his investment to be spent on players, Owen was manufacturing ways to grab it. Belokon summoned Owen and Karl to Riga to explain themselves, but they remained resolute in their refusal to admit they had broken the agreement.

The Oystons and their team continued in a remarkable act of intellectual contortion to justify the payment to Protoplan. In an internal email, accountant Ian Cherry wrote, 'When the club obtained promotion to the Premier League it was required to carry out a number of building projects including building a new stand.' This was either a lie or a mistake. Andrew Green pressed Owen on the issue under cross-examination. Owen wouldn't concede at first, but after a heavy reminder that he was under oath, he admitted there was no Premier League requirement to build anything. They needed to put together a media centre for the larger pool of press assembling for games, but this didn't necessitate construction work. In fact, the Oystons freely skirted other Premier League regulations. They were supposed to install new cabling through the stadium that TV cameras and crew could connect to. Karl hadn't gotten around to it until a member of staff blew the whistle. He only had the work done once the league refused to release central distribution money until it was sorted.

Still maintaining the falsehood they needed to build a new stand, Cherry went on to write, 'Due to the outstanding debt with Protoplan it was felt that it would be difficult, if not impossible, to find a firm willing to undertake this work if the previous construction work was not fully settled. The decision was made therefore to loan monies from BFC to Segesta to repay the Protoplan debt and fund the construction and upgrade of the stadium … I would point out that BFC are the main beneficiary … as without this work they would not be able to play in the Premier League and qualify for the substantial broadcasting payments and prize monies of around £100m which will follow. As such the funding of an outstanding trader debt to Protoplan seems a small price to pay.' This explanation was a fantasy. Even if building a new stand was a requirement, it made little sense that doing so relied upon repaying a loan from ten years ago – a loan that existed from one Oyston-owned company to another. The new East Stand was built and open for games before the Protoplan loan was even repaid, completely obliterating any retrospective justification. Nevertheless, Rod Dyer advised that in the Blackpool FC accounts, they should lump together the £4.2m loan to Segesta owed from 2000 and the £1.5m loan to build the East Stand in 2010 as one £5.7m payment. It would be titled the 'stadium development loan 2010', spin any politician would be proud of.

The attempt to obfuscate the payment was typical of the continuous disguising of money being taken out. The club's financial accounts, which were often filed late, were like a jumbled-up jigsaw missing the final pieces. Up next was a highly controversial series of transactions over the Travelodge hotel situated behind the Bloomfield Road stadium. The land had once been home to the Tangerine Nite Spot, a nightclub owned by Segesta until it burnt down.

The club and land came with the football club when Owen Oyston purchased it. In 2008, Segesta sold the now-empty land to another Oyston-owned company, and they built a Travelodge on it. He took out a five-year mortgage when developing the hotel. In February 2011, Owen Oyston emailed Karl to suggest paying off the mortgage early, making sure to write, 'The money would have to come from Segesta/Blackpool FC.' He need not have bothered with the possibility of it coming from Segesta. There was only one place it could come from.

By now, the Oyston side were becoming more brazen in carrying out such transactions without consulting Belokon and Malnacs. One email wrote, 'The loans will be informal and effected in the next two or three days, without any written documentation. This will avoid the months and months of toing and froing between the various parties.' The lack of formality and documentation also meant there was no requirement for repayment. Owen Oyston proposed that Blackpool FC lend Segesta £4.9m, so the company could pay off the mortgage and the early termination fee. For its part as the lender, BFC was entitled to nothing in return. Instead of sharing in a split of the Travelodge profits, Owen Oyston retained them all, about £450,000 per year. He offered to pay, entirely at his own discretion, £200,000 back to Blackpool FC for up to 50 years 'if he so wishes'. If paid in full it would net £10m, their money back plus a small amount of interest. The Oystons tried to argue in court it was a favourable deal. As usual, behind the flimsy façade, the benefit to Blackpool FC was non-existent. The loan was informal, with no security, at complete discretion to Owen Oyston.

Later in the 2010/11 season, Owen made further payments out of BFC to cover the full cost of the Travelodge, which had escalated in price. The deal now included stamp duty and VAT, totalling to £8.12m overall. Andrew Green eviscerated the transaction for the lack of commercial sense it made for Blackpool FC, the company stumping up the cash. Questioning Howard Belton, Owen's tax advisor, he asked, 'Is it normal for repayment terms worth millions of pounds to be at the discretion of the borrower, not the lender?' Belton erred slightly, before admitting that it wasn't. Then it was Karl's turn in the witness box. It had been six years since the loan was paid out of BFC, with an expected return of £200,000 per annum towards repayment with interest. 'How much has been paid?' Green asked. 'I have no idea,' Karl replied. 'How much interest has been repaid?' he asked instead. Karl again replied, 'I have no idea, I don't deal with those things.' Clifford Chance already had the list of financial transactions; Green wouldn't ask such a question if he didn't already know the answer, and he knew only £170,000 had been paid. That left nearly £1m still outstanding.

Karl tried to deflect the questioning on to financial controller Rod Dyer, but Green motioned him towards his earlier evidence, 'You said in your witness statement all the interest had been paid?' Karl feebly promised he would look into it, but at this point Green was unrelenting, 'Why has this only just come to light? This is a commercial arrangement and payments should have been made! How is this in the interests of Blackpool FC? Do you even care?' He had Karl rattled. The engagement was interrupted by the lunch break, before which Green had pestered Karl to investigate the missing payments. During the break Karl was scrambling around for ideas and he emailed Dyer to see if they could push through payments to satisfy the court.

As they returned, Green looked over at a couple of fans at the back. 'I hope you enjoyed that as much as I did, boys,' he smiled.

The last 'disguised dividend' was the £11m taken out in 2012 by Owen's company Zabaxe. This was the final straw and severed whatever relationship was left. There was little Belokon and his team could do to stop the payment, despite their protests over email. A simple vote at a board meeting overruled them. Malnacs and his predecessor, Kaspars Varpins, continued over the years to push the Oystons into more openness and transparency. They achieved little success. In a series of unsecured loans, £28m was transferred away from BFC into Segesta. Player wages and the continuing development of the stadium were given as explanations, but there was no way of verifying such claims. The cost of work on the stadium seemed exorbitant on the face of it. Fans questioned why the money couldn't stay in the club, if that's what it was being spent on. In a board meeting in 2012, Malnacs asked the same question. He was told that Owen Oyston was worried about the financial climate, and wanted to take the money out of BFC's NatWest account and place it into a Lloyds TSB account, as it had 'the healthiest balance sheet in the country'.

The money was transferred to Segesta's account, rather than simply opening up a new one in the name of Blackpool FC. Rod Dyer was asked why, by Fraser Campbell.

'There was absolutely nothing to stop, was there, Blackpool FC opening new accounts?'

'It's actually quite difficult for a football club to open bank accounts, believe it or not.'

'It's quite difficult ...'

'Yes.'

'... to approach a bank and say, "I've got £5m, could you accept it please?"'

The Oystons admitted to the court that £2.5m from the £28m had been used without benefit to Blackpool FC. The rest, they contended, had been put into the club. Clifford Chance didn't produce evidence beforehand to argue otherwise, so the judge took what the Oystons said as truth. He did, however, include the £2.5m in the running total for the disguised dividends he accused Owen of taking.

The case for the defence relied upon calling into question Belokon's credibility. In court, Blackpool fans gave him a hero's welcome. He was treated like a celebrity; they lined up for selfies and passed on words of encouragement. He knew how to play up to it. At one stage when giving an answer, his translator said the word 'orange', instead of the famous tangerine shirts Blackpool wore, a mistake any fan would be quick to jump on. Belokon did the same, and corrected his translator to say tangerine, in full view of the court. Every supporter who spent any time with him came away remarking how much of a pleasure it was to be in his company. He was polite and affable. He had only ever been the good guy in Blackpool's story. It was something magnanimously accepted by both Sam and Karl Oyston after the trial. Sam stated, 'Belokon has been an honourable bloke from the day he first put money into that club. My dad knows it, Owen knows it. Owen fucked him over well and truly. Belokon was more than entitled to what he wanted.' Karl added, 'He put money in. He funded a bit of a charge to the Championship. He funded the South Stand, which was definitely a bone of contention. He was part of the mix that got us to where we got, certainly as one of the board at the time. I think Valeri deserves to have the adulation in some regards ... I don't begrudge him a penny, or begrudge the adulation that he gets. He deserves both, frankly.' Owen turned down the opportunity to give his own thoughts and declined interview requests.

What neither his son nor grandson accepted, at least after the fact, was Owen's story that Belokon had made a death threat to him during a private dinner. It was during the Premier League season, the two had drunk lots of wine and the night was drawing to a close. Owen had a guest with him, a third party he claimed heard the entire encounter. The judge asked why he didn't call this witness to the stand, and Owen said he wanted to protect her privacy. It didn't take much reading between the lines to realise who his guest was, and what she was receiving in return for her company. The story went that Belokon was asking to be made full partner, now that the club had enough money to ensure that tax losses were no longer an issue. When Owen refused to answer, Belokon said, 'One way or another, I'll get my 50 per cent,' before leaning over to Owen's guest and remarking, 'Don't get too attached to Owen, he'll be dead within 12 months.'

Owen played it up, claiming he feared for his life. He called Belokon, who had served in Afghanistan for the Russian army, a 'crackshot sniper'. With the lack of any witnesses, at least in front of him, the judge had little reason to believe the event ever occurred. He questioned why, if such a 'bloodcurdling' threat had been made, the two continued doing business for several more years. Belokon strongly denied ever making such a comment, although others suspected he at least made a dark joke along those lines, in a state of heavy inebriation.

When it was his turn to perform cross-examination, Oyston's QC Alan Steinfeld was, by all accounts, a very competent and professional barrister. But he was playing with a bad hand and nobody thought he matched the performances of Green and Campbell. With the 'death threat' meeting given little appraisal by Justice Smith, his next-best tactic was challenging the source of Belokon's funding. He raised the money laundering convictions Belokon and his banks had. He asked why part of the money Belokon had invested was first loaned to his daughter, Vlada. Vlada had then made the investment on behalf of her father, although her role amounted to nothing more than a cypher. Belokon claimed this was done as a way of introducing her to the world of business, giving her some notional involvement in the deal. Steinfeld didn't hold back. 'Nonsense! You were trying to disguise the source of your funds!'

This was largely a new area of concern. There had been no claims of any wrongdoing by Belokon for the nearly ten years he was involved in Blackpool FC. The Oystons' shock and horror at his business dealings only surfaced once he initiated proceedings against them. Owen was happy to take his money as owner, and Karl was happy to spend it as chairman. It bought the players who took the club to the Premier League and funded long-overdue stadium construction. Fans referred to him as 'Uncle Val'. He was the perfect investor. He'd given them some money, but not enough where it felt like they'd bought their way to success. He'd seemingly asked for little in return, until now. He hadn't taken more than a couple of hundred thousand back in repayments from the stadium income, and a smaller share of the Charlie Adam sale than he'd been entitled to.

That there were legitimate questions surrounding Belokon and the financial world he came from, was as much an indictment of the lack of due diligence and moral compass the Oystons had in dealing with him. Belokon's Baltic International Bank (BIB) in Riga *had* been the subject of repeated investigations into money laundering. Nobody inside Blackpool FC cared. In 2011, Karl Oyston received a letter from a non-governmental organisation called Global Witness, which asked a series of questions regarding Belokon's background. He passed it on to Belokon's office, but otherwise left it ignored.

There is a pervasive idea that business conducted in eastern Europe is destined to be improper. Belokon was 29 years old at the fall of the Berlin Wall and he created a business empire in the murky wilderness of post-Soviet reconstruction. Nobody with that résumé is able to stay squeaky clean, even with the best of intentions. Such thinking gives startling benefit of doubt that has not been earned. In 2011, an investigation discovered that Belokon's bank in Riga had been used to launder nearly $700m through to Mexican drug cartels. It was again accused of money laundering in 2016, after a Latvian investigative journalism team presented evidence showing it was moving money out of the country into offshore bank accounts. Leaked documents showed that not only were they facilitating laundering and tax evasion, but they were actively promoting it. The bank handed out a cheat sheet guide on how to get away with money laundering to its interested clients, including tips on how to avoid red flags and mislead regulators. As part of a feeble crackdown attempt on Riga's banking sector, it was hit with a €1.1m fine. Belokon refuted allegations and promised to handle the matter internally.

Whatever actions they took, it wasn't enough. In 2019, another fine of €1.56m was imposed on BIB for their lax rules. They were punished for failing to uphold an 'adequate control system for the prevention of money laundering and terrorism financing'. Belokon's bank had no problem paying these fines. As long as such paltry sums are the only punishment, further allegations are hardly likely to go away. At various points over their relationship, the Oystons held millions of pounds of Blackpool FC's money in Baltic International Bank as a 'goodwill' gesture.

Belokon previously operated Manas Bank in the country of Kyrgyzstan, before it was seized by the state. While it was under his control, it was alleged to have taken money laundering to a whole new level. Belokon had formed a close business partnership with Maxim Bakiyev, the son of President Kurmanbek Bakiyev. Reports out of the country claimed that Maxim was actually a shadow owner of Blackpool FC, alleging he contributed money for Belokon's initial investment. The story gained little traction in the UK press, and Blackpool fans could be forgiven for never hearing about it – although most that did were far too occupied with the club's success to care. Maxim's friendship proved incredibly useful. Belokon was able to purchase the previously nationalised Manas bank in what was alleged to be a rigged process. Law required at least two separate bidders to make pitches, but Belokon's only competition was Maxim's personal friend and schoolmate, who had little proof of funds. There was a short deliberation process before Belokon was awarded rights to purchase Manas. Maxim Bakiyev took over the second floor as his own personal office space, rent-free.

Maxim's father, Kurmanbek Bakiyev, was the target of protests against his regime in 2010. Citizens took to the streets of the capital, shouting 'down with thieves!' Organised crime was flourishing under his presidency, and political instability was growing. Four politicians had been murdered in the few months following his election. After a day of protests turned violent, he fled the country. Armed guards met demonstrators and fired indiscriminately into the crowds. Over 80 people were killed, with 450 more wounded. Bakiyev was sentenced to life in prison for his role, although by this point he was hiding in Belarus. His son, Maxim, was also charged *in absentia* with embezzlement. He was in charge of the state development fund, a huge pot of cash mostly brought in from Russian aid, and then brought out in briefcases by Maxim and his cronies. He was accused of stealing $35m of the fund before he fled. It represented nearly one per cent of the country's entire GDP.

A British businessman called Sean Daley accused Maxim of hiring hitmen to kill him while he was working in Kyrgyzstan. He was brokering a deal over a gold mine which Bakiyev wanted to get his hands on. He was shot in the back four times, but fortunately survived. When he took the case to England's High Court, a key witness failed to show. The witness had previously claimed to have been in the room when Bakiyev was informed Daley survived, and heard him orchestrate a follow-up attack. He surely had a good reason not to show for testimony, for he was sentenced to jail for contempt of court. Daley lost his case. The witness was out of the country by then. It didn't take long for pictures to surface of him sitting in a new yacht he bought, following a report that he was paid off.

Soon after the protests which ousted his father, an audio recording of a phone call supposedly between Maxim and his uncle was leaked online. It revealed how they were planning to fund groups to initiate violence, giving them money and weapons to conduct riots. It showed the level to which the

Bakiyevs would go to in order to maintain their grip on the country. Maxim wanted swift action, 'These 300–500 people must not go with stones in their hands, they must be well-equipped. Otherwise they'll be dispersed and shot down. It should be done … Cruelly, suddenly and quickly! We must tell each of them, here is two or three thousand for you. Do it and you'll be given as many again!' Horrific waves of violence did indeed break out and Human Rights Watch described the scenes on the ground as 'pogroms'. There was brutal violence for four days. Entire villages were swept through. Men were tortured and killed; women attacked in gang rapes. The police, filled with men thought to be loyal to Bakiyev, watched on. In some cases, they joined in. Around 100,000 people fled across the border and 400,000 refugees were displaced from their homes, which were looted and burnt down. This is what Maxim Bakiyev funded. This was the man that Valeri Belokon was doing business with. The two still remain in contact.

Belokon refutes any claims of wrongdoing by his friend as propaganda. Together, they incorporated a company called Maval Aktivi, using the portmanteau of their names. It was created with the intention of investing in new business opportunities outside of Kyrgyzstan. Belokon and Bakiyev owned 50 per cent each. One of the businesses they invested in was VB Football Assets, the company set up with the purpose of acquiring shares in Blackpool FC. In 2006, VBFA paid Blackpool FC £2.8m as part of the price of Belokon's purchase. In the same year, Maval Aktivi loaned VBFA the exact same amount. There was nothing written on paper, no document or acknowledgement when it came to Blackpool FC, to suggest Maxim Bakiyev had just become a new minority owner. Few within the club knew of his name until journalists came asking about the connection, and he certainly wasn't involving himself in the operations. However, in court Belokon could not recollect the purpose of the £2.8m loan from Maval Aktivi. He had no answer as to why the exact sum of money he'd used to purchase shares was transferred from a joint venture with Bakiyev. For his part, Bakiyev certainly wanted people back home in Kyrgyzstan to know he was the proud new owner of a British football club. One ex-associate, who was particularly close with him at the time, stated, 'Maxim had strongly intimated that he was a partner in the club.' Local reports often referred to him as part-owner, as did a US diplomat in a leaked cable to the State Department.

As part of a large delegation of guests invited by Belokon, Maxim travelled to Bloomfield Road for Blackpool's first home game after his investment, and posed for a picture overlooking the pitch with his business partner. There was a suggestion made in court that he had also met with Owen Oyston in the Premier League season, although it is unclear if this is true. Bakiyev had by then claimed asylum in England, as the government rolled out the blood-red carpet for a man on the Interpol wanted list at the time of his entry. Maval Aktivi loaned VBFA another sum of £2.5m in 2008. At the same time – coincidentally, as Valeri Belokon pleads – VBFA transferred the exact same figure into Blackpool FC, after signing an agreement to fund construction of the new South Stand. In court, Oyston's counsel offered this as part of their defence, but Justice Smith moved the line of questioning along. He also made a point of ignoring Belokon's conviction for money laundering in Kyrgyzstan, where he had been sentenced to 20 years in prison. This wasn't particularly surprising, as the country's reputation is hardly one of openness and transparency, and Belokon didn't even submit a defence. However, the decision was upheld in the more reputable Court of Appeal of Paris, where Belokon had taken the chance to fight his corner with Clifford Chance.

More evidence emerged of Belokon's improper financial dealings – of a bank account for a company in New Zealand held by a Belarusian taxi driver, carrying out transactions worth hundreds of millions of dollars, and of another company sitting on millions in his bank, owned by a 20-year-old who had never been to Kyrgyzstan, and was in prison at the time. While any Blackpool fan deserved the right to know who owned their club and where the money came from, neither Bakiyev's supposed involvement nor Belokon's financial history were established as relevant to the case. It didn't stop Steinfeld from ham-fistedly trying to force it in questioning, but he was rapped on the knuckles for doing so. It would have mattered little anyway. The judge concluded, 'The mere fact that the petitioner is a wrongdoer, even in relation to the company of which he is a member, is not enough to deny him or her remedy.' It dealt a large puncture to the Oystons' defence.

The evidence of their unfair prejudice towards Belokon was substantial. Email after email flew between the Oystons and their advisors, with no consideration to the minority shareholder. Latvia was rarely included in discussions. They disapproved of every single one of the 'disguised dividends' taken out of the club, but their objections were overruled. The judge concluded what the fans already knew, 'Owen Oyston's plan seems to have been to identify debts owed by Segesta to other companies in the Oyston Group, and to treat these obligations as obligations to be discharged by Blackpool FC.' Midway through the hearing, Justice Smith asked both sides to consider what remedy they would suggest if he ruled in Belokon's favour. It was the first big hint that he was winning.

Once the case concluded, once every witness had been dispatched from the stand and sermons were given in closing arguments, all that was left was to wait. It was an agonising four-month wait, extending past the late summer recess of the courts. In early November, the day came. Sixty Blackpool fans packed the courthouse. Standing room only. As they walked up the steps and into the building, there was an atmosphere of excitement and anticipation, fuelled by sides of beer at breakfast. The Oystons didn't bother to show up. Their legal team looked particularly glum, while Clifford Chance were sporting big smiles. The verdict had been delivered to them beforehand, behind closed doors. Owen's private investigator, Les Goulding, commented to one fan, 'I think you'll like what you hear today.' So, they started passing around numbers. How big could it get? How much could the Oystons afford to pay? They counted assets on their fingers, could they sell them before having to sell the football club? Whatever the verdict, it wasn't going to be a declaration that the Oystons had to sell Blackpool FC. But if the compensation was big enough, they might be forced into it. Everyone settled down into the room. The judge walked past and took up his seat. He began the legal talk. It was a summation of what he'd already told both sides privately, it wasn't a dramatic speech for the audience.

Then he mentioned the figure – £31.26 million. The judge continued on, soundtracked by dozens of fans tapping on their phones, their glass screens practically burning to the heat of the surface of the sun. The room was abuzz with the vibrations of notifications. The messages from thousands more fans back home, celebrating in unison. There were double takes of incredulity in the audience. 'Thirty-one million?!' they mouthed to each other. Stephen Sharpe, one of those sued by the Oystons, was sat amongst them. He turned to the person next to him and whispered in his ear, 'They can't pay that.'

Chapter 8

Aftermath

AT THE old Number 1 club, in the same room where Karl had mocked the ten fans at the SISA meeting, hundreds more turned up to celebrate the victory. A smaller group cramped together on the staircase up to the second-floor room, trying to hear what was being said through the packed crowd. Tim Fielding entered to a standing ovation. While he'd left his role as chair of BST some years ago, he was still looked to as a leader. Nobody had been affected more personally over the last six years than he had. He'd been targeted and sued by the Oystons for alleging improper financial dealings, only for a judge to declare they had 'illegitimately stripped' Blackpool FC of £26.77m. He'd worked tirelessly, in whatever spare hours he had away from the office, to find a solution. He met with potential bidders, liaised with Valeri Belokon and Kaspars Varpins in Latvia, all while being a voice for the fans and representing their plight in the media.

It was a jubilant atmosphere. They raised glasses and sang songs commemorating their battle. They looked to the future, but Fielding had a word of caution. It wasn't the end. More patience was needed. Owen Oyston could find the money he owed Belokon without selling the football club. If he did, it would leave a distressed asset and an owner with no more money to put in, even if he wanted to. Everything would be back to square one. Worse, in fact. There would be no great court case on the horizon to save them this time. The Latvians had warned him that there was nothing they could do to enforce the sale of the club. If Owen had the money to pay, they had to accept it. Fielding's biggest fear was that Owen might secure a loan to pay off Belokon. His concern was well placed. Despite his advanced age, a portfolio of businesses that were almost exclusively loss-making, not to mention the defence he had promoted in the court case where he claimed his business partner was a money launderer, Owen was able to secure a loan and pay £10m to Belokon, the first tranche owed.

He needed to pay the second £10m instalment a month and a half later. He was going to have to sell off assets to get the money, but from day one, Owen was failing to comply with the judge's order. There were reportedly over 60 people or groups who expressed interest in purchasing Blackpool FC, although the vast majority were chancers – parties looking to loan money to fund the purchase, only to flip it later. Owen wasn't interested in listening anyway. He was seen attending games with John Disley, the so-called 'King of Marbella', known for leading an extravagantly tacky champagne lifestyle on the Costa del Sol, and spending years in prison for fraud. Although he'd won an appeal against his conviction, fans feared they were about to go out of the frying pan and into the fire.

Belokon's conviction in Paris meant he was ineligible to take-over. Those fans who worked with him had long hoped he would one day buy the club. It was a particularly cruel blow. They had spent so long petitioning the EFL to disqualify Oyston, and now the same rules were being used to ban the one person they hoped could save it. There were suggestions that Belokon would appeal the decision, but over time his enthusiasm seemed to diminish. He'd just gone through a costly divorce with his ex-wife. The prospect of pumping more millions into a football club didn't seem as enticing as it once did.

With the court case resolved, there was nothing left holding together the Oyston family. Owen and Karl had fallen out in the build-up to the proceedings. In meetings with lawyers, Karl begged his dad to listen to their advice. Owen would explode, 'Fuck off, you deal with these idiots then!' and leave. Karl would work with the team afterwards, only for Owen to return an hour later and undermine everything they had worked on. Karl was also working with Normunds Malnacs on last-minute negotiations. The day before the court case started they had come to a figure of £9m, which Valeri gave the green light on. However, Owen wouldn't sign off on it. After the hearing, when it was obvious to most observers that Belokon had won, if not by how much, more settlement negotiations took place. Belokon travelled to Owen's villa in Spain to see if the two could shake hands on a deal, but Owen was still unable to come to terms with the reality of what was happening. The details of exactly what number was on the table at what specific date are hazy for all those involved. A figure of £7.5m has been floated, although it is unclear whether this was available before or after the hearing. Belokon said at one stage he would have gone as low as £6m. These were not figures Owen would entertain. Instead, even after the case had concluded, at the meeting in Spain, a source with knowledge of the situation said he was trying to get Belokon to invest *more* money in the club. At one point back at his offices he was overheard shouting, 'I'm not giving that man a single penny, he single-handedly ruined the club!'

Everyone around Owen was pleading with him to strike a deal. His own wife and son were both telling him he was never going to get a better offer. But there was never any convincing Owen Oyston that he couldn't secure better terms. He had built a career and a life off promoting himself as a cunning businessman. He had, for years, squashed smaller businesses and contractors who he left with empty pockets. He went after fans who didn't have the resources to fight back. But Valeri Belokon was one person he couldn't bully. The deal fell apart. A few weeks later, Marcus Smith delivered the result nobody could possibly have dared to hope for – £31.26m plus costs. Not even Clifford Chance had expected it. They had no inclination whatsoever that even the best outcome would net such a huge return.

For Karl, that was the end. He had no interest in being a party to his dad's antics. He wrote to Belokon's solicitors and the court to explain he no longer wished to be associated with him. He suspected Owen of writing emails and expressing opinions under the façade of being from both of them, behind his back. The family were trying to distance themselves from Owen once they realised he wasn't going to comply with the directive to find the money. Karl claims he put the club on the market two days after the judgment, but Owen wouldn't listen to offers. He claimed one bidder offered to pay more than twice as much as it was eventually sold for, but he dug his heels in and refused.

Owen gave his ex-wife, Vicki, a gold bar for a Christmas present. Around the same time, he had asked to borrow a spade. Family members questioned why a man in his 80s, who had never done a day's gardening in his life, suddenly needed a spade. They joked he was digging up gold bars he had buried in fields around Blackpool, although one was adamant it wasn't a joke. His finances should have been effectively frozen. He had a debt to pay of close to £40m once court fees were included. Yet he was still giving money to other family members he was still close with, to help fund their lifestyles. Blackpool fans, once so jubilant after the victory in court, anxiously waited for the day they could return to the stadium and watch their team. It was a frustrating period of stasis.

After Karl told Owen he had written to the other side, effectively giving up dirt on him, Owen sought his revenge. He suspended Karl as chairman and put Karl's sister Natalie in charge. Then he went after his own grandchildren. That included Sam and his sister. The latter he threatened to kick out of her home, the former he actually did. Sam was also put through a disciplinary process at the hotel. Owen produced a 50-page 'dossier' of complaints against him, accusing him of stealing. For his part, Sam claimed this was partially true; he'd taken money out of the safe, but it was all accounted for. He alleged Owen would regularly ask him to grab bundles of cash to take for himself so he could throw it around town at his boozy dinners. Owen declined several requests for comment for this book, but a source within his team corroborated this account, saying at one point Sam got so fed up with Owen's demands to pay restaurant bills and expense it later, that he resorted to carrying expense forms for him to fill in there and then. It wasn't illegal, it was all signed for, he was just doing what his grandad had asked him to do. 'Why the hell would I, if I was stealing money, sign for the money?' Sam asked. He was sacked, but immediately started proceedings against the football club and Owen for unfair dismissal.

The process was delayed once movement finally came with a new board taking over. Without confirmation from anyone involved – nobody would either confirm or deny the story – it's obvious to conclude that Sam received a settlement figure from the new ownership of the club. It's likely that Karl did too, after he also initiated proceedings for unfair dismissal and the withholding of wages. When Karl arrived at the tribunal court he was greeted by a guard of honour. Blackpool fans lined the corridor, taking photos and selfies as he walked down. As everyone waited for the hearing to start, he was put in a room with fans, who couldn't believe their luck. One asked a security guard why he had placed them together. 'Because I'm a football fan,' he replied. Karl went right up to the window, looking out, determined to ignore the jibes and the photo taking behind him. Jeremy Smith, the man Karl and his father had tried to sue, came up to the window and stood next to him. He offered one sole comment. 'It's funny how life works out, isn't it Karl?'

Meanwhile, Owen Oyston was hauled in front of court again, to explain why he'd failed to pay the second instalment of £10m he owed. The judge questioned why certain assets were being put on the market at inflated valuations. One house, valued at £250,000 by Owen himself, was listed with another for £600,000. He criticised the lack of transparency in their efforts. Owen's team asked for more time to come up with the money, claiming they were close to securing another loan. They presented a statement by a manager of a finance group, which read, 'I have now obtained terms for a loan of £10m from a company that manages loan activities for an offshore investor. This is a formal offer, which we are proceeding with now.' However, the judge noted that in the terms of the offer it was written, 'You should not enter into any financial commitments based on this in-principle offer.' He concluded, 'This is very far from a formal offer.' No extension was given and Owen had to pay up.

The deadline came and went; £25m plus interest and other costs remained outstanding. Belokon and his team discussed whether or not to petition the court to install a receiver, a third party tasked with a single mandate – to take over and sell the assets for the best possible price. They feared what this might mean for Blackpool, as it had never been done before in British football. The EFL had strong disciplinary measures for clubs that went into administration, slapping down 12-point deductions as punishment. At the start of the 2018/19 season, still competing in League One, Blackpool were flying high in the table. But around Christmas they hit a poor run of form and the prospect of a 12-point deduction began to bring up relegation concerns. Belokon and Kaspars Varpins deliberated on the decision, worried what the fans might think if they were the reason such a punishment came. 'You have to do it,' Tim Fielding argued. Many would have accepted a drop all the way down to non-league football if only it meant they could watch their team play. Getting rid of the Oystons was the only thing they cared about. They would start from the very bottom and rebuild if they had to.

Results picked up over the following weeks and the threat of relegation ceded to a worry that a deduction would knock Blackpool out of their play-off push. Nevertheless, with the backing of the fans they consulted with, Belokon had Clifford Chance formally request to the court that a receiver be put in – that the judge forcibly remove Owen Oyston from the club. For one last time, fans descended on the court for the hearing. It had been 14 months since they sat together and heard the £31m awarded to Valeri Belokon. Even then, they knew the story hadn't ended. They knew there was a wait to come; victory had not yet been achieved.

As the hearing to appoint a receiver proceeded, it looked to be going the wrong way. Before the lunch break, Justice Smith warned Clifford Chance they had to do more to convince him. Fielding whispered to fellow fan Scott Koudellas, 'This isn't looking good, I don't think we're going to get a result here.' It was a small room, with the audience in close proximity to the lawyers. As Koudellas craned his neck over, he could see Owen's legal team passing notes to one another. They had a new QC arguing the case, and he passed a note back to one of Owen's relatives, watching on. On it, he'd written, 'We've got this, we've won.'

Koudellas had been to an earlier hearing that he hoped would deal with the football club, but all that was discussed was some property in Fleetwood. He was annoyed at how slow the whole thing was. He'd taken holiday at work and booked travel to watch, only to see a debate over two houses that had nothing to do with Blackpool FC. The judge had ruled in favour of Oyston that day over the two properties. At the end of proceedings, their QC came up to Koudellas and Stephen Sharpe, who he was also sat with. 'I make that 2-0, boys,' he bragged. 'How did you work that out?' they replied, 'More like 14 fucking two!' 'Oh, what did you give me the two for?' the lawyer asked. 'One for winning some crappy houses and the other for managing to spell Belokon's name right!'

Koudellas and the other fans watching on didn't have much longer to wait, but early indications didn't look good. Smith declined to install a receiver for Owen's non-football assets, citing a lack of evidence that it was necessary. That left the football club and its associated properties. In front of all the fans in the back who had been painfully sacrificing for years, and in front of BST chair Christine Seddon, who had been a driving force behind the 'Not A Penny More' campaign, the judge gave them their validation. He reasoned that the protests and boycotts would continue to have an adverse effect on the value of the club. With fans staying away from the ground, refusing to buy tickets and merchandise, the asset was not attractive to a potential bidder. On that basis, he made the single most important action that had been made at Blackpool FC in half a decade. He removed Owen Oyston and the board from the club and appointed Paul Cooper and David Rubin as receivers. He gave them one direct order, to sell the club for the best price they could get. Without the effort of the fans, he might never have done so.

Some had wanted Owen out the day he bought the club. For others, it took longer. Fan protests took hold in the 90s. There was a coffin march, and the famous image of a car parked outside the ground all painted in tangerine with anti-Oyston sentiment written on had become etched into the club's history. There had been a period of acceptance and even optimism in the 2000s; Belokon came aboard and with his money, Ian Holloway's team took them to the promised land. They had their legacy robbed from them, shattered and devoured by a greedy family with little care for what football meant to ordinary people. In the words of ex-Liverpool managing director Christian Purslow, 'Blackpool are the only club in the history of the Premier League who didn't give their manager a chance or spend anything. They just trousered the money and said sod it, we'll go straight back down.' After 22 years, the Oyston name was stricken from Bloomfield Road. Thrown aside and relegated to history. All that was left was the future, however uncertain.

Those who had followed along had deified Marcus Smith ever since he'd delivered his judgment on the original case. That he made a point to reference their boycotting efforts was the validation that made everything worth it. He was an Arsenal fan. From day one he had a great understanding of what the Oystons had done, and what it meant not just for the football club, but the community. As he walked out of the courtroom, Stephen Sharpe stood up and shouted, 'Up the Gunners!' Smith laughed as he walked past. Then Owen's QC exited. 'You're getting sacked in the morning!' the fans chanted. They celebrated like they hadn't since that blazing hot day in May at Wembley in 2010. They cheered the names of Marcus Smith, Andrew Green and Fraser Campbell as loud as they had Brett Ormerod, DJ Campbell and Charlie Adam. They did it all the way home to Blackpool with cans of beer thrust into the air. Then the work started.

Paul Cooper set about appointing an interim board, and decided early he wanted a fan to be included. He settled on either Tim Fielding or Christine Seddon. They both decided that Tim should take the role, although Christine was later hired as general manager at the club hotel. She had worked at Hilton hotels for 36 years and her experience was needed to bring it up to scratch.

They faced challenges immediately. Days before they came in, Owen had his staff remove or destroy financial documents. One person referred to it as the 'shredathon'; it was like a plague of locusts going through each office room at the stadium. Through his intermediaries, Owen had instructed senior members of staff to stay at home and not report to work. Staff who did come in were unsure of what to do, fearing punishment if they co-operated with the new interim board. Owen produced two leases which he claimed had been in place beforehand, giving him and his company the ownership of office space in one of the stands, as well as the penthouse above the club hotel. The validity of these leases is now being questioned. Up to the time of writing, Blackpool FC are embroiled in a battle which will likely soon play out in court to recover these leases. They have had a difficult time fully separating the Oyston family from the stadium.

After spending some time away in Spain, Owen has been seen coming and going from the penthouse. His daughter Heidi is currently still living there, and it is believed the club is taking steps to remove them. Further, they are investigating a transfer of close to £1m which was made out of the club the day before the receivers came in, which Owen should have been in no position to make. The £36m in intra-group loans that left Blackpool FC were all written off in the period leading up to the receivership. The loans will never be recovered. Since selling the club, Owen has turned his ire to the latest people he felt had wronged him. He took legal action against the receivers over their fees, which he ultimately lost.

Work commenced immediately to repair issues at the stadium, with the homecoming game two weeks away. For the first time in years, thousands upon thousands of fans were going to flock to Bloomfield Road to watch the team's next home match against Southend. The video screen didn't work and needed fixing up. Volunteers came to the stadium to help clean up pigeon poo that hadn't been cleared for years, cobbling together whatever supplies they could gather and getting to work. On his first day, Tim Fielding took a tour of the stadium and looked on in disgust at what had become of it. Anywhere Owen didn't walk in his daily routine had been left mostly abandoned. There was junk everywhere. The kitchen made him feel physically sick. The sinks had mould all around them and the floors were dirty. When equipment broke down, the old staff would grab bits of gear from elsewhere in the kitchen and try to replace it, rather than paying for proper repairs. The whole place was crumbling to bits. The Oystons hadn't invested into the running costs in recent years.

The receivership had limited financial means to make improvements. The only real income came from the rent payments from the Travelodge hotel, which they also had control over. However, Paul Cooper and the interim board had at least managed to persuade the EFL that they were solvent enough to avoid the points deduction. The rule existed as a retroactive punishment for clubs that overspent to gain an advantage. Such an advantage clearly didn't exist at Blackpool. They were also somewhat lucky in that the club had virtually no debt. It was a completely unique situation. The only comparative cases were the clubs that had administrators appointed after going bust, with creditors lining up to bang the door down and recover whatever money they were owed. For Blackpool, the existing liabilities were manageable. Transfer fees still being paid off to other clubs were small, and other than that it was just gate receipts from matchday that had to be shared out. As long as the staff were paid and the lights were kept on, the operation was able to run smoothly. By showing the EFL that everybody was getting what they were due, in a timely matter, Cooper dissuaded them from taking any action. It alleviated much of the outside distraction and pressure, and instantly gained good favour from the fans.

At the hotel, Christine Seddon was having her own problems. She realised soon enough just how dangerous the place had become. The equipment wasn't working. Health and safety checks hadn't been properly carried out. What little money there was to spend was going to the football club first, but with hard-working people, who had proper experience and the right qualifications, they brought it up to scratch. Just like inside the stadium, no financial documents had been left for them. They didn't even operate a proper lodger book. Owen would invite guests in at a whim, with no information input into any sort of internal system. It was a mess. There was nothing to go off. As she walked into the office at the back of the hotel, Seddon was rifling through papers when she found a random stack of money, £5,000 in cash lying between files. As she considered everything around her, the enormity of the situation dawned. The stories she was hearing from inside the stadium only confirmed those thoughts. A few more weeks was all it might have taken and they wouldn't have had a football club to come home to. 'It was teetering on the edge. In terms of the structure of the place, the lack of any kind of investment over any period of time. The simple fact is, they'd been taking out and taking out, nothing had been going in. You can't continue to maintain something like that in a safe fashion.'

The first two weeks were about cleaning and sourcing new equipment. Seddon feared a trip from the environmental health services. If they had seen what was left for them, they would have shut it down. She brought in an expert cleaner who asked to open up the extractor fan above the cookers. The fan led to a vent that travelled all the way through the roof of the restaurant, underneath the hotel rooms. It was thick with layers of grease. They require thorough cleaning twice annually, but this one hadn't been cleaned in years. The reason she knew was because nobody had bothered to install any access panels. It was a fire risk, right underneath all the rooms. She had to wait a week for it all to be cleaned, and couldn't sleep properly until the job was done.

The next priority was putting proper discipline and HR rules in place, to prevent the sort of stories that had been coming out of the hotel for years from repeating themselves. 'It was like the wild west,' Seddon remarked. She said staff members informed her that the young women who worked at the hotel would mingle with players freely after their shift, while prostitutes came and went on a regular basis. Rules were put in place and properly enforced to create a safer and more professional atmosphere. Sam Oyston claimed his staff would never dare to get involved with players when he was there, having left a year earlier.

The new interim board and small army of volunteers got the club into shape for the first home game back. Preparations were still ongoing right up until matchday. They didn't have card reader machines so Fielding had to run around at the last minute to source some. He was practically begging local suppliers for food to use in the hospitality boxes. But then, homecoming day finally did come. It was a game on a Saturday afternoon that ended

2-2. Blackpool finished 10th and Southend finished 19th. It was one game of 45 more that weekend in the Football League, with over half a million people all convening in their spiritual homes to watch. And now Blackpool fans were among them. Packing out Bloomfield Road, never letting up their singing and rejoicing. It didn't matter when Southend went 1-0 up. It didn't matter when they retook the lead at 2-1. It didn't even really matter when Blackpool scored a 97th-minute equaliser courtesy of an own goal, although the footballing gods clearly enjoyed writing the flourish for the end. It was what was happening in the stands. Stranger hugging stranger, releasing pure joy and emotion. What mattered was simply that they were together.

Epilogue

FEW IN Blackpool had even heard of Simon Sadler before he bought the club for £9m in June 2019. He hadn't met with BST while they were holding meetings with interested parties, nor had he made any real overtures in the years before the 2017 court case about buying out the Oystons. But he was watching, from afar. He was a lifelong fan. The story spread that Sadler was the owner of Stanley Matthews' 1953 FA Cup winner's medal

Born and raised in Blackpool, he had left to build his fortune in Hong Kong, where he has lived for the last 20 years. The timing had to be just right, and it was. Football clubs rarely turn a profit. Unless you are one of the lucky few to play in the Premier League, the escalating costs of player wages and transfer fees are hard to cover from matchday income and trickled-down TV money alone. To commit properly to being a custodian of a club requires a high level of dedication – not just with time, but with money. By 2019, Sadler was ready. He was the only bidder that made sense. He combined a good price with a mountain of paperwork and thorough due diligence. He talked a good game with his vision for supporting the local community and followed it up with action.

With his right-hand man, Brett Gerrity, they got to work repairing the relationships that had broken with local businesses. He wrote large cheques to cover running costs and renovations to the rusting stadium, not to mention new signings. Gerrity and Sadler had met as two 19-year-old lads, working on Blackpool beach hiring out deckchairs for the council. It was a well sought-after summer job for students. There, they spent whole days together, working in tandem. They passed the time by talking about life and grand plans for the future. They built a close relationship which has lasted ever since. Gerrity describes Sadler as a genius. He never had any doubt he would be anything less than a huge success, in whatever he put his mind to.

Owen Oyston threatened him with a lawsuit when he made his bid, but he carried on undeterred. He petitioned the court to relieve Oyston of the 20 per cent stake he owned through Valeri's old shares – which he'd technically been ordered to buy for the £31m he eventually did pay in full. Sadler refused to carry out the purchase if an Oyston was involved. The judge obliged. He gives little away to the press; he is described as an intensely private family man. He delegates to the people he trusts and oversees from afar. Soon after the purchase, at a local pub where a few fans had gathered, Stephen Sharpe got a tap on the shoulder. 'Are you Sharpey?' he was asked. 'I just want to say you deserve a medal, your posts on the message boards have kept us going these last few years.' It was Brett Gerrity, he was talking about himself and Sadler.

Sadler joined the players in celebration on the Wembley pitch in May 2021, as they lifted the League One play-off final trophy after a thoroughly deserved win over Lincoln. Two years after his purchase, he had taken the club back to the Championship. A team with exciting, young talent, playing attractive and winning football, watched by the Blackpool fans that were able to make it into the reduced-capacity stadium. Also there that day was Derek Spence, the man who had built the Community Trust charity and had left once the club started suing fans, citing the toxicity working for the Oystons as the reason he had to undertake four years of counselling. One evening, his wife had called him into the kitchen, telling him he'd gotten a letter from the football club. When he opened it, it was two VIP tickets to Wembley for the final. In two decades working at Blackpool, the Oystons had never once invited him to a game or offered him complimentary tickets. Simon Sadler, who had never met Spence, who had taken over after Spence had left, had seen to it that he be rewarded with two tickets for himself and his wife. When he was sat at his kitchen table that night, he burst into tears.

COVID-19 had forced most of the season to be played to an empty stadium. But the fanbase had waited for so long, they could wait for one more year. Now back in the Championship, it feels like the soul of the club has returned. Internally, Blackpool officials believe manager Neil Critchley, who had previously worked in the youth set-up at Liverpool, to be the finest developer of young players in Britain. A quiet, assured man, he speaks confidently and honestly to the press. The fans adore him. They adore their players. They ambush the Australian national football team's Twitter account to vote en masse for their recently called-up bleached blond-haired midfielder, Kenny Dougall – the 'King' who scored both goals at Wembley – to win man of the match in online polls. Even when he's on the bench. They awaited the summer reveal of the new season's kit, expressing love or hate and buying it anyway. They hear of a young player from another team's under-18s that they might be buying, and convince themselves he's the next big thing. They warn off rival supporters on social media that their 20-goal striker Jerry Yates will never leave. They do all the things football fans are supposed to do.

At the time of writing, Blackpool are enjoying a good run of form after a shaky start to the season. Once it's out in the world, they might be pushing for a second consecutive promotion. Or, they might be scrapping near the bottom for survival. Or, they could be headed towards a completely bland, mid-table finish. I will be watching with my dad. Either at the ground, or through shared messages on the family group chat. I will be watching with the man who brought me up a Blackpool fan and sat next to me for so many years before we joined the boycott. Together, we will share once more the joy of football with our loved ones. That was something I once took for granted. Now, I realise it is a gift.